D0427542

RoadMap

*how to understand,
diagnose, and fix
your organization*

by

N. Dean Meyer

SECOND EDITION

RoadMap: how to understand, diagnose, and fix your organization

Meyer, N. Dean

Key words: reengineering, transformation, leadership, organizational structure, organizational design, organizational health, organizational systems, teamwork, culture.

NDMA Publishing
641 Danbury Road, Suite D
Ridgefield, CT 06877 USA

203-431-0029
ndma@ndma.com

ISBN   0-9641635-2-7

Printed in the United States of America.

*A good constitution
is infinitely better
than the best despot.*

— Thomas Babington Macaulay —
First Baron of Rothley
(1800-1859)

BOOKS BY N. DEAN MEYER

Decentralization: Fantasies, Failings, and Fundamentals. 1998.

Why decentralization is so expensive and harmful, and how to get the benefits without paying the costs.

Structural Cybernetics: An Overview. 1995.

The science of designing entrepreneurial organization charts and building dynamic, cross-boundary teamwork.

The Information Edge with Mary E. Boone. 1987.

How to find and measure the strategic benefits of information systems (with over sixty case studies).

In memory of
Mimi.

CONTENTS

FIGURES

RoadMap

*how to understand,
diagnose, and fix
your organization*

FOREWORD

People want to do a good job.

But much too often, the organizational environment they work in gets in their way. At a minimum, this wastes people's talents and energies, and puts impossible loads on executives. At the worst, it induces people to perform poorly, work at cross purposes, fight with one another, and burn out.

Meanwhile, organizations are facing tough challenges from their competition and from a volatile, complex business environment. If everyone in an organization isn't doing everything possible to assure its success, the organization is doomed to mediocrity or even failure.

This book describes a straightforward approach to building healthy organizations — ones in which everybody's talents are fully engaged and their independent actions are well orchestrated.

It is a handbook for executives who are disappointed with quick fixes, jaded about management fads, and fed up with solving the same problems day after day . . . for leaders who are tired of fighting alligators and ready to drain the swamp.

PREFACE: Engaging Every Bright Mind

The first responsibility of a leader
is to define responsibility.
The last is to say thank you.
In between, the leader is a servant.

— Max De Pree —

Tough competition from every corner of the globe. A mind-boggling pace of technological change. Acquisition threats and opportunities. A legal and regulatory environment that constrains every move. Unpredictable markets. Demanding customers. Consolidations. Change!

Organizations are swamped. And the pressure is on leaders to achieve unprecedented and ever-increasing levels of performance despite unyielding obstacles.

Many traditional leadership strategies aren't working. Pep talks and forcing people to work harder only serve to reduce productivity by alienating workers. Training and team-building feel good, but the results rarely live up to expectations.

Industrial engineering (now called business process reengineering) cuts costs in the short term, but leaves behind rigid assembly lines, unimaginative environments, and demotivated staff who are treated as automata within carefully engineered procedures forced on them by efficiency experts.

In its extreme, the slash-and-burn mentality of the monomaniacal cost cutter is especially shortsighted. While it delivers short-term savings, it chases away the best talent, severely damages effectiveness and flexibility, and puts companies in a death spiral.

As one colleague said, "Approaches which failed in the past are even less likely to succeed now."

And after all these attempts to improve organizations' performance, the "management fad of the month" has people either terrified or, perhaps worse, laughing at executives and cynical about change.

Perhaps it's time to revisit the fundamentals. How do organizations work, and what makes them perform well?

To analyze why organizations perform well or poorly, we must first define the term "organization." Our definition must accommodate all types of leadership situations, both entire companies and internal service departments ("staff" functions) that, as businesses within a business, feel all the same pressures and face the same challenges.

An "organization" is any group of people working together to achieve a common and ongoing purpose (line of business) which benefits people outside their profession. It may be a corporation or a company, a government agency, a union, a family working on their farm, a volunteer association, or a service department within a company. It may seek to make a profit, or it may be not-for-profit.

Organizations exist to serve "clients" — people who benefit from their products and services. If the organization is a company, its clients are customers external to the company. If the organization is a department within a company, its clients are, for the most part, other employees within the company. *1*

---

1.   We use the word "client" differently from "customer." Clients are customers outside an organization who buy its products and services. Another group within an organization may also buy a group's products, add value, and then pass them along to a client. Thus, a client is one type of customer, but other groups within one's own organization may also be customers.

Some of the pressures organizations face originate from demanding clients and tough competition. Other pressures result from changes in the business environment. Still others are the product of friction within organizations.

An "organization" may be a company or a service department within a company.

Amidst all the myriad pressures on organizations, one thing is clear: Executives who "take control" and personally make all key decisions become bottlenecks that bring organizations to a standstill. Executives' traditional roles of high-level decision makers and master project managers are stifling everybody else's creativity and their organizations' performance.

To deal with all the many tough challenges organizations face, there's only one answer: empowerment.

As badly overused as the term "empowerment" may be, one fact remains: Organizations cannot afford to waste one iota of talent. Organizations won't survive unless every bright mind is engaged, both individually and in teams, in assuring success.

Empowerment is not a fad or a nicety; it is a necessary response to the immense pace and complexity of today's business environment.

Unfortunately, most attempts at empowerment fail. If empower-ment means anarchy, organizations will fall apart. Of course, executives cannot let this happen. When they see badly implemented empowerment leading to chaos, executives must step in and again take the reins. "Oh well," they say. "We tried empowerment; it didn't work. What's next?"

But executives cannot afford to give up on empowerment. They just have to learn to do it right.

Executives who "take control" and personally make all key decisions become bottlenecks.

To understand the difficulty of empowerment, imagine that the overall goals of the company are clear. What mechanism will get everybody in the company to work in concert to achieve those shared goals? Conversely, why is it that people work at cross-purposes even when they share common goals?

For organizations to work — that is, for them to perform any better than an equal number of individuals — people must be coordinated. They need clear and integrated priorities, accountabilities, and authorities.

Furthermore, controls are necessary, not because people are stupid or evil, but because organizations must ensure that their scarce resources are used for just the right things, and that people's activities are aligned with organizational goals.

In the past, managers played a critical role in coordinating and controlling people's work. This put managers in the position of bottleneck while wasting many of the bright minds in organizations. Eliminating the management bottleneck means one thing: abandoning the organizational hierarchy as a means of coordination and control.

Empowerment dismantles one mechanism of coordination and control, specifically, top-down management. But somehow, people's daily activities must still be coordinated. You can't just say, "Okay, everybody, here's a common goal. Do as you see fit." Common goals are necessary, but in themselves don't coordinate people's daily work. Meanwhile, "do as you see fit" means that management will no longer serve as the coordinating mechanism.

In other words, you cannot dismantle one mechanism of coordination and control without explicitly replacing it with another. Effective empowerment depends on replacing hierarchical coordination and control with some other coordinating mechanism.

Empowerment requires coordinating mechanisms other than the management telling people what to do.

In healthy organizations, controls are not a matter of micromanaging bosses and occasional audits, but rather are inherent in what people must do to succeed. People are managed based on their results; and they determine for themselves how to achieve those results. Coordination and control are built into the definition of "results."

Put another way, empowerment doesn't mean eliminating controls; it means moving controls from the top line to the bottom line, so that people are managed by results rather than by tasks.

In such an environment, people can act independently. As they look after their own success, they will automatically do what's right for the organization as a whole. And executives can stop "micromanaging," that is, directing tasks and intervening in day-to-day decisions. They won't need to. Instead, managers can focus on adjusting the organizational signals that guide everybody every day.

Empowerment doesn't mean eliminating the organization chart, getting rid of managers, or undermining the chain of command. It means getting managers *out* of the job of telling people what to do, and *into* the job of leading organizations.

What is leadership? First and foremost, it's a matter of designing healthy organizations.

As an alternative to hierarchy, coordination can be built into the fabric of an organization. Organizations send signals that guide everybody's behavior. In a healthy organization, these signals are well-aligned, so that individual initiatives are *automatically* well coordinated.

"Healthy" organizations send signals that guide everybody's behavior, so that their individual initiatives are automatically well coordinated.

Of course, getting all the signals right in an organizational environment is not simple. It requires a thorough understanding of the mechanisms within organizations that influence people. This is a core competence of leaders.

This book describes how leaders can implement empowered, high-performance organizations without chaos. It's not a quick fix. It's not a magic pill that solves every problem. It's not a standard prescription that works the same in every company. Rather, it's a way of thinking and a science of organizational design.

RoadMap is a comprehensive framework that helps leaders focus on the fundamentals of organizational health, as well as a straightforward participative planning process that leads to transformational change.

THE CHALLENGE

*The nation will find it very hard
to look up to the leaders who are
keeping their ears to the ground.*

— Winston Churchill —

1. Pat's Predicament

Perhaps some portion of Pat's story will ring true for you . . . .

Pat was appointed the head of a large organization. To get acquainted with the situation, she embarked on a series of interviews with both key clients and a cross-section of her staff. Here's what she found:

Clients said that Pat's organization is pretty good at providing traditional operational services and conventional products. They recognize that Pat's products and services are an operational necessity, but do not think of them as a strategic resource and don't feel that they are particularly relevant to top executives. As a result, they don't consider Pat's organization to be their business partner.

Even for traditional products and services, clients view Pat's organization as unresponsive to their needs. They don't seem to know where in the organization to go for what. At times, they even feel the organization is an obstacle to their doing what they need to.

Client executives feel that Pat's organization is not customer focused. They are annoyed by frequent misunderstandings between Pat's staff and theirs. They complained that Pat's people don't listen to them and don't seem to care about their problems. Sometimes, people in her organization are arrogant and think they know better than their clients how to run the clients' business. Occasionally, they even attempt to dictate what clients should do with the clients' own money!

Clients are also concerned that Pat's organization can't seem to complete projects on time or on budget.

Furthermore, they are aware of the rapidly changing technologies of

Pat's industry, and sense that the organization is not sufficiently innovative and that it's falling behind its competitors.

Of particular concern, clients think that Pat's organization is too expensive, and they're not sure where their money is going. Worse, to get her organization to do their projects requires a convoluted, bureaucratic process that often feels like begging. As a result, clients feel that her organization is out of their control. Some are even contemplating finding another vendor. (In the case of internal service functions, this means outsourcing.)

Pat's interviews with her staff were also disturbing. People love the company and believe in its products. But they don't have a real sense of identity with their own group's business. As a result, they focus on tasks rather than results, and don't feel empowered to be creative. Some are afraid to speak up. Many just do as they're told. Most are demotivated. One even got up and left mid-way through a meeting with Pat because it was quitting time!

Staff are also annoyed by the frequent misunderstandings with their clients; but they don't feel that it's their fault.

People generally feel overworked and underappreciated. They get upset with clients for expecting more and more, and for making unrealistic demands without giving them the time and the resources they need to do a good job.

Working so hard to please clients, people have virtually no time for professional development or experimentation with new technologies and techniques, so their skills are becoming obsolete. As if this weren't bad enough, they are further demoralized whenever contractors are brought in to do the innovative, new work that they'd like to learn to do.

People enjoy their peers, but rarely form teams across organizational boundaries. When they do, teamwork is often marred by confusion over accountabilities and resources.

As a result of all these factors, productivity is low, turnover is high, and recruiting needed talent is difficult.

In summary, Pat emerges from her interviews with the following concerns:

* Lack of strategic alignment.

* Overcommitted, leading to lack of responsiveness and people feeling overworked.

* Lack of customer focus, in part due to unclear agreements.

* Unreliable project delivery.

* High costs.

* Lack of innovation.

* Clients feel out of control of priorities.

* Lack of staff identity with their business, leading people to focus on tasks rather than results.

* Lack of teamwork across organizational boundaries.

Why would an organization that succeeded for so many years now seem so troubled.

And more importantly, what should Pat do?

To answer these questions, we must first take stock of the business environment and the many tough challenges that leaders face.

2. It's a Different World

Organizations face pressures far beyond anything they have experienced in the past. Many leaders, like Pat, feel unprepared for the challenges. Their concerns are well founded, as a brief historic perspective shows.

The familiar 1950s slogan, "I like Ike!" (referring to U.S.-President Dwight D. "Ike" Eisenhower) may invoke nostalgia for a simpler past: the post-World-War-II economy with its steady growth, seemingly unlimited resources, and competition constrained to a few well-known adversaries, for the most part within national boundaries. During that era, it may have been safe to assume that "the future will be just like the past, only more so!"

The relatively simple and predictable business environment of that time encouraged people to equate the word "strategic" with "long term," and to focus business strategies on a few key goals. Executives developed three- to five-year plans, and presided over their implementation by forming project teams, determining assignments, setting priorities, and monitoring results. Organizations prospered, fortunes were made, and executives were able to personally know enough to manage all the business details. Everything worked fine, until . . . .

In the last quarter of the twentieth century, the world changed in fundamental ways. Now competition is global, resources are severely constrained, the economy is highly volatile, the regulatory environment in convoluted, customers are ever more demanding, and technologies have grown in complexity beyond the grasp of any single individual.

In this new world, the concept of strategy has taken on a different meaning. Instead of meaning narrowly-focused and long-term, "strategy" now means the *variety* of new things that an organization must do *right now* to prosper.

In short, the world is no longer simple and stable.

This fundamental change in the business environment has precipitated a crisis in organizations and in leadership.

Organizations that did a good job in the simpler business environments of past decades may not be equipped to address the challenges of today's complex, volatile world.

"Strategy" means the variety of new things that an organization must do right now to prosper.

No organization is exempt from these forces. While changes are particularly noticeable in industries which are growing rapidly or deregulating, every business is facing ever-tougher competition. When one company feels the heat, they demand more of their suppliers, and business pressures ripple backward through the value chain. Even regulated utilities and governments are under pressure to perform at formerly unimagined levels.

All these challenges apply both to whole companies and to internal service functions within companies. As line managers learn to meet their external clients' expectations, they demand more of their internal service providers. As a result, the pressures of the new business environment affect every functional area of every business.

In fact, internal service functions are particularly sensitive to these forces. Departments that may have succeeded in the past as "necessary evils" are finding their monopolies evaporating in the face of decentralization and outsourcing, but may not be ready to earn the status of line management's strategic partner.

It's clear that leaders of both corporations and the departments within them are facing entirely new challenges.

3. The Bar Has Been Raised

Before delving into how to ready organizations to deal with this changed world, let's take stock of the new demands being placed on organizations.

What, precisely, is expected of a successful organization in this tough business environment? Or, put another way, exactly what is meant by the widely used term, "world class"?

Since every organization offers a unique product line, "world-class" performance must be defined at a level higher than specific deliverables. It means superior performance in every aspect of its work.

In the most general sense, there are two types of performance: efficiency in routine operational tasks (gained through productivity improvements and cost savings), and effectiveness in creative tasks (reflected in quality, flexibility, customer focus, and innovation). Both must be delivered year after year in a rapidly changing business environment.

This definition of performance, while comprehensive, is still vague. To take it to the next level of detail, consider the expectations arising from five fundamental changes in the business environment:

* **Agility:** A volatile business environment demands that organizations be capable of rapid shifts in their strategies, as well as of commitment to traditional long-term visions.

* **Intimacy:** Clients expect their suppliers to invest in partnerships, to know them well, and to contribute directly to their strategies.

* **Diversity:** While people have in common many aspects of their administrative work, missions are diverse; and based on their unique missions, individuals and small groups sign up for

unique business strategies. This means that organizations must tailor their offerings to each unique client.

*   **Competitiveness:** Increased competition means that organizations must learn to do traditional tasks much more efficiently and better.

*   **Competence:** The competition for talented employees has grown fierce, and attracting and retaining good people is extremely difficult.

Each of these changes in the business environment demands new levels of performance from organizations. Let's examine what is expected of organizations in response to each of these challenges.

Agility

With the volatile nature of business strategy, long-term plans are obsolete shortly after they are written. Over-emphasis on planning can damage an organization's responsiveness. Instead, organizations must learn to grab windows of opportunity and formulate strategies on the fly. Strategic planning must not be a once-a-year event; it must be a continual, dynamic process.

Flexibility must extend to an organization's finances and capacity. If clients want to spend more than was planned, a world-class organization expands its supply to match funded demand. In the short term, capacity can generally be augmented through the use of vendors and contractors. In the long term, every organization must forecast its market and develop its infrastructure in advance of clients' demands. If capacity is not expanded, clients will either resent the organization as a constraint to their businesses, or they will simply take their money elsewhere.

And, of course, a fast-paced world demands a high pace of innovation. In order to beat their competitors to market with new concepts and technologies, most organizations must reduce the time from ideas to marketable products (the "cycle time").

Intimacy

Clients expect a close partnership with their suppliers — a relationship built on service and mutual respect. Strategic partnerships extend beyond a simple commitment to doing business together. In partnerships, suppliers are expected to contribute directly to clients' business strategies.

First and foremost, a world-class organization must serve, not control, its clients. While this is obvious to companies which must compete in the open market for business, internal service functions often attempt to use monopolies and policies to disempower business units. A world-class service function, on the other hand, guides clients by earning their business and their respect, not by inhibiting or opposing them.

An organization must lift clients' vision of the business value of its products and services, and help clients understand how to use its products and services in a strategic manner. This amounts to a marketing mission, as relevant to internal service functions as it is to whole companies.

An organization must help individual clients diagnose their business strategies and discover high-payoff opportunities to apply its products and services. Too often, organizations settle into a comfortable "order-taking" mentality. But it's not enough to satisfy clients' demands. Value is created at the very beginning, before a job is defined, when clients decide what products and services to buy and how to use them.

An organization can ensure its strategic alignment by actively facilitating this initial diagnostic process. It must help clients discover strategic applications, envision new business strategies enabled by their products, and justify investments based on strategic value (not just cost savings).

Note that this does not mean that an organization should decide on behalf of clients what products and services to produce. A world-class organization proactively helps clients discover opportunities for themselves, and then responds to their purchase decisions.

Finding a linkage between clients' business strategies and an organization's products is, essentially, sales in the very best sense of the profession. Sales is as relevant to an internal service department as it is to any business as a whole. Both must proactively help clients succeed by facilitating a strategy-driven discovery process.

An organization can also add value by helping various clients discover common interests, and facilitating the formation of client consortia to share solutions. This not only saves clients money; it builds synergies among business units.

To help clients make the best use of its products and services, an organization is expected to support its product line with training, customer service, and repair. Furthermore, as strategic partnerships grow, clients expect added-value services that give them a competitive advantage, such as just-in-time delivery or custom electronic data interchange (E.D.I.). In other words, clients demand "mass customization" — i.e., the quality and service of custom products at the price of mass production.

Of course, an organization must form clear agreements (contracts) with clients, and must fulfill every agreement. To meet every commitment, it must never make a commitment it cannot keep.

Since clients are the beneficiaries, they must take responsibility for justifying the products and services they use. Within corporations, a service function must help clients defend the budget for its products and services (even if the budget is channeled directly to the service organization).

Similarly, an internal service function must help *clients* set priorities within its available resources. Too often, internal service departments are given a fixed budget and then expected to do everything clients ask of them all year. Of course, this is impossible, and clients become frustrated with staff deciding priorities and repeatedly telling them no. A world-class organization makes clear to clients what resources are available to them, and then helps clients make purchase decisions within available resources.

Diversity

Each corporation has a unique position in its market, and hence a unique set of strategies. Furthermore, each client has a unique mission, and hence a unique role in the corporation's strategies. To align with clients' strategies, organizations must focus on what is *different* about clients, not what they all have in common.

Organizations must dispel the "one-size-fits-all" mentality. Common solutions address common problems, and typically all that every client has in common is administrative work.

To deliver strategic value, an organization must customize solutions to fit clients' unique needs, rather than just build commodity or companywide solutions. Tailoring products and services is essential to strategic alignment.

To respond to unique clients' needs, an organization is expected to offer a broad product line. Providers that wish to remain their customers' primary source have no choice but to be full-service vendors that offer the broadest possible range of products and services. If the product line is limited, clients will develop the habit of buying from competitors.

Furthermore, a limited product line forces an organization to become "a solution in search of a problem." Conversely, organizations that offer a broad range of products can focus on solving clients' business problems in a business-driven rather than product-driven manner, and provide whatever products are needed to address their clients' unique needs.

Similarly, offering a range of qualities and levels of value allows clients to select a price-point appropriate to their needs.

Even in small organizations, a broad product line is essential. Of course, it's quite all right to broaden one's product line through partnerships with vendors. This is far better than sending clients to competitors or appearing product driven.

Beyond offering a diversity of products, when considering a particular client's request, an organization is expected to offer options. With each option, an organization must give clients all the information they need to choose. This is the opposite of an internal service function that makes decisions for its clients since "they know their profession best." It's the essence of customer focus.

Competitiveness

In addition to learning new skills to align themselves with clients strategies, organizations must respond to increasing competitive pressures. Global competition is forcing once-complacent companies to dramatically increase their performance. Similarly, internal service functions are facing tough competition in the form of outsourcing and decentralization, and can no longer rest on the laurels of past monopolies.

Clients' increasing reliance on partnerships brings increased scrutiny of their suppliers. WalMart, for example, examines its suppliers' financial practices and makes "suggestions," such as the elimination of corporate jets and reductions in executive compensation, to bring their prices down.

Similarly, within corporations, everyone is interested in "helping" managers of internal service functions manage their businesses. Organizations can no longer say, "This is too complex for you to understand . . . . Leave the decision to us." Instead, it must run its businesses in an open, impeccable manner.

In increasingly competitive markets, every organization must find a way to "do more with less." It must do everything in its power to keep its prices (i.e., costs) competitive.

At the same time, amidst burgeoning technological change, an organization must proactively keep its products and services up to date. Continual investment in innovation is essential to delivering competitive value, and to staying in business.

In every product area, organizations are expected to offer world-class quality. Defects drive clients' costs up, and damage clients' reputations. While every product need not be "gold plated," quality must consistently meet clients' expectations.

One aspect of quality is product-line integration. Integration gives clients greater flexibility to mix-and-match products, and the ability to quickly change configurations as their business needs change. It also reduces support costs. Beyond cost savings, integration can create business synergies as an organization's products help clients collaborate with each other.

In spite of technological diversity and unique customer requirements, providers in most industries are expected to design products to work well together. In product design, an organization must both create diverse solutions and, at the same time, integrate its product line by utilizing standards and reusable components.

Competence

In every facet of business, greater complexity demands a greater degree and diversity of specialized talent. More than anything else, people create an organization's competitive advantage.

To attract and retain a qualified staff, an organization is expected to provide a safe, supportive work environment. It must give people well-focused jobs that don't ask them to be experts at too many things at once. Jobs must be "whole," such that people are accountable for product lines (rather than roles or tasks). And it must support staff in their professional growth with challenging work assignments and opportunities for professional development.

In Summary

To use the sport of high-jumping as a metaphor, "The bar has been raised." The pace and complexity of business have grown by orders of magnitude. As a result, ever more is expected of organizations — of both entire businesses and the service functions within them.

Succeeding at strategic alignment in a volatile, competitive business environment requires dramatically higher levels of performance.

The above is just a sampling of the many performance expectations of competitive organizations. Both clients and staff are demanding things of organizations that were unimagined in the past.

Clearly, no organization can claim to be excellent at all these things. Nonetheless, this long list of demands is far from unrealistic. "World class" is not just a motivational slogan. Quantum leaps in performance are necessary to survival.

To prosper in turbulent times, organizations must limber up and get in shape. Businesses must learn to be flexible, opportunistic, and capable of numerous simultaneous initiatives.

4. The Paradoxes of Success

Responding to the challenges of a tough business environment is not just a matter of working harder or more efficiently. Hidden within the expectations described in Chapter 3 are a number of paradoxes that force leaders to rethink the way organizations work.

Consider the following examples:

Diversity and Integration

To offer a broad range of products amidst the burgeoning complexity of technologies, organizations must draw together experts in a far broader range of disciplines than ever before.

In spite of this diversity, organizations must also integrate the various technological components into a coherent product line.

These two pressures are diametrically opposed. The more diverse the technologies, the tougher it is to integrate them.

Integration and Responsiveness

Organizations are expected to offer an integrated product line. The commonly suggested answer to the need for integration is a top-down "plan" that designs the entire product line all at once. To do this, organizations scan the range of technologies and narrow them down to a subset that can be integrated.

At the same time, organizations are expected to deliver strategic value to their clients. Strategic solutions are, by necessity, tailored (customized) to fit a particular client who has a unique mission and a unique business problem.

But top-down plans only address problems which everybody in the company or the market *shares*. Since only administrative challenges are common to everybody, top-down plans rarely result in products tailored to clients' specific strategic opportunities.

Furthermore, long-term plans don't respond to clients' rapidly changing business strategies. And yet, without planning, it's difficult to integrate an organization's various products.

Organizations are expected to integrate diverse technologies, and simultaneously offer clients strategic solutions tailored to their unique, here-and-now needs. Again, these objectives appear paradoxical.

Saving Money and Investing

There is another paradox inherent in the focus on strategic value.

Clients expect solutions that directly contribute in significant ways to their missions and the key business imperatives of the company (strategic value), rather than just indirectly through administrative cost savings.

Yet, simultaneously, clients often question the return on investments in the organization's products. Their concern is natural. Success requires careful cost control, often steering people away from investments in lucrative areas of strategic opportunity (a false economy).

How can people view an organization's products as strategic, and at the same time consider it a target for cost-reduction?

Business-driven and Technology-driven

Many high-tech organizations traditionally have been rich with technology gurus, but weak on business experts.

The need for a focus on technology has not diminished. Organizations must be leaders in technology to generate new product opportunities. In fact, the need for technical excellence is greater than ever in the face of growing technological complexity and pace of change.

At the same time, organizations must be business-driven (not technology-driven) in their approach to clients. They must provide insights into the strategic use of their products, and design tailored solutions *after* fully understanding clients' business needs. Without significantly expanded business skills, the promise of strategic value will be elusive.

Paradoxically, organizations must be both business-driven and technology-driven. These two very different perspectives require different skills and different kinds of people.

Success requires a careful balance of conflicting forces, and dynamic processes that continually adjust the balances.

Change and Stability

Organizations must continually invent new products and manufacturing techniques. At the same time, they must keep existing operations stable and support existing customers efficiently.

The invention process inevitably disrupts the smooth operations that benefit from stability. For this reason, it's quite rational for people who are responsible for stable operations to resist the fundamental changes brought about by new inventions.

Somehow, organizations must be both inventive and stable.

No Escape

As impossible as they might seem, these expectations represent the reality of today's business pressures. To survive in a competitive world, organizations cannot afford to fail at any of their often-conflicting missions.

Doing more of the same, somewhat more quickly and efficiently, will not address these paradoxes. Characteristically different organizational processes are needed to both pursue excellence in each area of endeavor, and, at the sime time, to continually adjust the balance of numerous paradoxical forces.

5. The Answer: Organizational Health

With the tremendous pressures on today's organizations and the many tough (and often paradoxical) expectations they face, "doing a good job" is tougher than ever before.

Unfortunately, few organizations are reliably performing well, year after year.

The problem isn't the people. Every organization has a range of talents. And no organization can bet its future on hiring only super-achievers.

The problem isn't resources either. Increasing the budget of an organization is likely to produce more of the same, not new kinds of results.

And the problem isn't technology. A new tool or technique makes an organization more efficient at what it chooses to do, but it won't help an organization make the right choices. In fact, sometimes a new technology can make an organization very good at doing the wrong things.

The problem is much deeper than any of these. The problem just may be an obsolete organization.

What kind of organizations can handle the demands of a chaotic business environment? Or, put another way, what are the characteristics of a "healthy" organization?

First and foremost, healthy organizations do not waste any talent. *Everyone is fully engaged.* People feel accountable for a part of the business, and are in control of their business-within-a-business as empowered entrepreneurs.

Entrepreneurs are customer focused because they clearly understand that they must earn their clients' business to survive. Naturally, they focus on delivering results (products) rather than performing tasks.

Since they think like entrepreneurs in a competitive market, *everybody always looks for efficiencies* and new ways to satisfy their customers. And quality is a natural outcome because small groups of people are responsible for every aspect of producing specific products of the organization.

Well-designed, healthy organizations use every bit of their available talent.

Not only are people fully engaged, individually expressing their initiative and creativity as they work on a diversity of issues, but also *people are well coordinated* with one another. In healthy organizations, high-performance teamwork is a natural way of doing business.

Teams form spontaneously (without the need for management intervention) across organizational boundaries, because everybody is empowered to get the help they need from others. In this way, *cross-boundary teams are self-forming,* without waiting for management to assign staff to projects.

Since everybody knows just what help they need from others, *teams involve just the right people at just the right time.* Teams are not made of a fixed group for an entire project. Rather, people join teams for specific periods of time to contribute specific deliverables. In this way, a healthy organization *always deploys its talents in the optimal way.*

People ask others for help based on the unique needs of each project. The result: Processes are dynamic and tailored to the needs of each project, and *everybody automatically plans the most efficient work flows.*

This approach to teamwork is much more powerful than appointing a few "process owners" who disempower others by telling them how to do their jobs. And it's much more flexible than a single business process for every occasion (as in business process reengineering).

When seeking others' help, people contract for specific deliverables (rather than just "join my team"). This ensures that *people within teams are clear about their respective accountabilities.*

Furthermore, the chain of command is well established, since everybody knows who their internal customers and suppliers are. Thus, there is *no confusion about who's in charge.*

As a result of clear accountabilities for results and a clear chain of command, *teams are self-managing.*

In healthy organizations, high-performance teamwork is the normal way of doing business.

Also, contracting for specific deliverables means that team members manage their own pieces of the project. *Managing large projects is much easier,* since project-management responsibilities are distributed.

In short, high-performance teamwork is the normal way of doing business.

In a healthy organization, altruism is not needed. When the signals that guide people's behavior are well aligned, *personal success is achieved precisely by doing what's best for clients and the organization as a whole.* That includes working with others in the organization who bring unique skills and resources to the team.

With all its talent employed in a coordinated manner, healthy organizations achieve a *dynamic balance among the various paradoxical objectives.* Different perspectives take precedence at different times, as situations warrant.

For example, a well-established product line may require operational stability with continual, but marginal, product improvements. Operations may take the lead as the entrepreneurship that produces this particular product, and it subcontracts to designers for help with improvements.

On the other hand, a new product requires a flexible, inventive team. For this situation, designers may be in charge, while operations serves as their subcontractor.

Healthy organizations focus everybody
on the right issues at the right time,
and coordinate them with a
minimal need for management intervention.

With a high degree of customer focus and flexible processes, healthy organizations are *quick to adjust to changing client requirements and business strategies.*

By eliciting the best performance from every one of its members while coordinating their work, healthy organizations continually work at peak performance, continually adapt to a changing world, and continually evolve and improve themselves.

On the other hand, unhealthy organizations build conflicts into the very fabric of the work environment. They are filled with untenable jobs, fail to align people's efforts with clients' business needs, waste significant management time resolving internal political issues, and burn people out.

Organizations can make or break people.

As critical as they are to people's success, rarely have organizations been consciously designed to handle today's multiplicity of often-conflicting objectives, and to maintain excellence in the face of ever-more-complex technologies and rapidly changing business needs.

It's not that organizational health is an executive's only concern. Certainly every executive faces problems which are the result of causes other than organizational design, such as poor business strategies, inadequate resources and technologies, or incapable people.

But insightful strategies, adequate resources, innovative technologies, and great people do little good in unhealthy organizations. If dysfunctions are built into an organizational environment, other remedial actions will have little effect, since capable people may not put the remedies to good use.

Organizational health is so critical that it warrants a special position within an executive's personal leadership strategy. Any executive who wishes to improve people's performance should first address organizational issues.

LEADERSHIP

*The significant problems we have
cannot be solved at the same level of thinking
we were at when we created them.*

— Albert Einstein —

6. The Case of the Old-fashioned Foreman

To achieve the ambitious goal of organizational health in a fundamentally different, challenging business environment, an executive's role must change dramatically from past models.

Traditionally, executives were trained to determine strategies, make tough decisions, lead key projects, and manage by personally guiding people throughout the organization. These "top-down" executives have become bottlenecks, slowing their organizations down, limiting people's ability to respond to diverse strategic imperatives, and wasting much of their organization's talent.

An all-too-familiar example of this outdated style of management came from a high-technology equipment manufacturing company. The company had grown rapidly into worldwide markets, and its aging data processing systems could not handle the increased demands for throughput, flexibility, and integration. A companywide reengineering process confirmed that a complete revamp of all their operational data processing applications was warranted to keep pace with the growth of the business.

The former I.S. executive was stuck on mainframes, resistant to change, and continually battling clients. A new Chief Information Officer (C.I.O.) was hired from a prominent consulting firm to replace him and bring the department up to date.

Under the direction of the new C.I.O., a complex, multi-application package was acquired, and the I.S. department embarked on its worldwide roll-out with an aggressive multi-year plan.

Although the C.I.O. made sure that this very important project proceeded on course, everything else got worse rather than better.

Problem 1: The organization could not be trusted to fulfill its commitments.

The C.I.O. was very effective at selling creative ideas, but lacked in-depth technical knowledge. Obviously, no individual can keep up with a complex field like I.S.

When discussing new ideas with clients, time and cost estimates were based on his limited personal knowledge of what it takes to develop systems. The C.I.O.'s estimates did not benefit from the rest of the staff's much deeper understanding of technical difficulties, existing systems which had to be converted or integrated, the effort involved in the worldwide roll-out, other commitments (such as keeping the current business running), and people's respective abilities and learning curves.

By calling all the shots, the C.I.O. repeatedly made promises the department could not keep. His favorite phrase was, "We'll take care of that." In one case, he even promised a major application to Manufacturing although there was absolutely no time or budget available for the project.

As a result, a senior manager said, "You never knew what was going to hit you." Although the worldwide roll-out was the department's top priority and remained on schedule, the department soon earned a reputation for being untrustworthy.

Root cause: Instead of designing processes by which the organization could manage resources and commitments and respond flexibly to clients' changing priorities, the C.I.O. personally managed supply and demand.

Problem 2: The project was not well managed and took longer than it needed to.

Not trusting his staff, the C.I.O. periodically got involved in details of projects, thereby disempowering the project team with his decision making. But because of his time limitations and lack of technical depth, the C.I.O. could not know enough to make the right decisions.

No one person could. The worldwide roll-out alone was too big and complex for any individual to completely understand. Add to that the diversity of technologies, other projects, operational requirements, and business issues, and it becomes clear that even a genius could not know enough to make every decision.

By intervening in decisions for which he was ill equipped, the C.I.O. found himself changing direction frequently in response to newly discovered information. He would attend a project meeting, make a snap judgment, then change his mind the next day when someone caught him in the hallway and made a case for a different approach. Of course, the result was a great deal of time and effort wasted.

Root cause: Rather than improving the organization's ability to manage projects and involve all the right experts in decisions (e.g., by defining roles, processes, and methods), the C.I.O. personally managed project details.

Problem 3: Completed projects were rejected by clients.

The C.I.O. thought that he was hired to modernize technologies. As a result, he came up with project ideas, justified investments, set priorities, and initiated projects — all on his own. The investments he proposed were approved because he was very good at selling his ideas. This led to projects that lacked client sponsorship.

To make matters worse, he made key design decisions with a minimum of client input. In one case, he convinced the company to invest in a major sales prospecting system. When it was delivered, people in the field found it difficult to use, and it didn't do the things they needed it to do. As a result, they refused to use it, and a lot of money was wasted redesigning the newly-installed system to make it acceptable to the sales force.

Root cause: Instead of building a customer-focused, business-driven organization, the C.I.O. usurped clients' prerogatives and made decisions that clients should have made.

Problem 4: Relationships with staff were badly strained.

Assuming that he knew more than anyone else, the C.I.O. became so absorbed in managing tasks and so overwhelmed with details that he thought of nothing else (a "heads down" demeanor). With no time or energy left for people, he did nothing to develop his staff.

In fact, he did just the opposite. The C.I.O. was cold, distant, harsh, and even hostile. Working relationships were not based on openness and trust. People became defensive and closed, and were afraid to speak up. In return, they let the C.I.O. sink without offering their help.

Root cause: The C.I.O. isolated himself by focusing on doing a few projects rather than building a team that could do many projects effectively.

Problem 5: Wasting talent wasted money.

The C.I.O. blamed incumbents for the poor performance of the organization (rather than examining the organizational environment that constrained them). Since he didn't trust his management team, he hired friends into senior management positions. And, of course, in the hiring process, he ignored the opinion of the incumbents who had a much deeper understanding of the necessary technical qualifications.

As a result, these expensive newcomers lacked technical depth and background in the company, and were not very productive. Most did not stay long. Meanwhile, the people they displaced were not permitted to contribute their ideas, and some good people were forced out of the company (a waste of talent and money).

Similarly, rather than get people within the department up to speed on new technologies, the C.I.O. preferred hiring consultants to do the innovative, new work. This was expensive, and led to a dependence on outsiders that was self-perpetuating.

Root cause: Instead of utilizing all the talent within the organization, the C.I.O. thought he and a few expensive friends could do everything themselves.

The Bottom Line

This C.I.O. may have been a decision maker, but he was not a leader. He did nothing to ensure that the organization was able to carry out his decisions. He blamed people for poor performance, rather than the organizational environment that was strewn with obstacles to people's performance. He ignored the extensive knowledge in the organization, thinking that he knew better than his staff. And since everything had to funnel through him, he became the constraint.

Instead of leading people, this executive tried to succeed in spite of people. When he was asked to leave, the company found itself with an organization that was less capable of delivering business value than it was when he had arrived.

7. Leaders versus Managers

Put simply, the model of the executive as a command-and-control-oriented "foreman" is obsolete. In a business environment that is rapidly changing on many fronts, there's never enough time for one person to know and manage everything. Under a foreman-style executive, the pace of an organization slows, and it cannot handle the diversity of challenges it faces.

A small step forward is the executive who empowers people and then solves problems as they arise. Most executives enjoy solving problems; it feels good to get something tangible done. But solving problems is not enough. Executives cannot afford to work example-at-a-time. If they focus on today's problems, they'll be too busy to figure out how to prevent future problems (which, it seems, can always be postponed). Worse, they may become too close to the problems to see the "forest for the trees."

In addition to solving problems, executives must fix the organization so that similar problems do not recur, or at least do not rise to the executives' level.

Of course, there are times when executives must step into the day-to-day operations and fix a severe problem. But executives can never have enough time to solve every new problem. And executives who repeatedly "rescue the situation," and do no more, inevitably institutionalize their organizations' dependence on them.

Executives must also supervise people, a day-to-day task. "Growing" good people has a tremendous impact. But as important as it is, coaching individuals is painfully slow as a channel for change.

The problem with firefighting and people management is the lack of *leverage*. It may be fun to make tough decisions and lead the charge on critical projects. But that places far too much emphasis on only one mind: the executive's.

The most effective executives tap *all* the bright minds in their organizations rather than depend solely on the one at the top. Effective executives empower people at every level while guiding them toward individual excellence and high-performance teamwork.

The most important job of an executive is to design an organization in which everyone can succeed.

This captures the essence of the word "leadership" — in contrast to an executive's managerial duties. The managerial portion of the job is the time spent supervising people and doing the day-to-day work of the organization. The leadership portion is the time executives spend improving the way their organizations operate.

Managers supervise people and do the day-to-day work of organizations.
Leaders improve the way organizations do their day-to-day work.

Managers develop "strategic" plans that deal with the issues of the day. Leaders develop "meta-plans" that grow healthy organizations capable of dealing with the myriad strategic issues of today and tomorrow.

Managers envision the future of the business. Leaders envision organizations that will deal with whatever the future may bring.

Managers fight alligators. Leaders drain the swamp.

Figure 1 juxtaposes some of the tasks of leaders versus managers.

To illustrate the difference between managers and leaders, imagine that you are concerned about your organization's lack of partnership with clients. You would like people to focus on clients' strategies rather than just on traditional operational issues. You determine that there are three key activities that will make or break the strategic value of your organization: opportunity identification, clients' priority setting, and project delivery.

Opportunity identification: While it may be tempting for you to personally work with client executives to identify their strategic needs, it would not be good leadership. Your organization would be limited to the few strategic projects that you can find in the little time you can afford to spend with individual clients.

As a leader, you might introduce methods to identify clients' strategic opportunities, then let the organization find them day after day. When the organization continually works to ensure alignment, the result is an avalanche of projects well focused on the unique strategic needs of each client.

Priority setting: An organization's bottom-line value to clients is directly related to its priority-setting processes. If it pursues low-payoff projects, there is little staff can do to align their efforts with clients' strategies.

Within a company, a service department's executive may feel well qualified to determine project priorities on behalf of the company, perhaps with the help of an advisory committee. Typically, such committees meet for a few hours each quarter, and don't have time to understand the hundreds of creative ideas generated throughout the company (some of which cannot afford to wait months for a priority decision). As a result, "hot" strategic projects may not get done. Or worse, priorities are set once a year in a "strategic plan," and the organization becomes unresponsive to changes in the business throughout the year.

A leader, on the other hand, designs processes whereby clients dynamically adjust priorities throughout the year. As a result, clients are in control of their purchases; decisions are based on clients' much better understanding of their unique business needs; and priorities can shift as quickly as the business environment changes.

Similarly, vendors which help their clients become "smart buyers" of their products — and understand the relative returns on various investments — will deliver more value to their clients' bottom line than those which simply take orders.

Project delivery: In the past, the boss formed project teams and supervised their work. However, in a dynamic organization, dozens of projects are initiated each month. Each requires a unique mix of skills and a unique sequence of activities. The boss may not understand exactly what skills are needed when; and, without the right talent on each team, productivity will suffer.

Business process reengineering, while it may be a step forward, is still not leadership. Executives who reengineer the product-delivery process, for example, are working at the level of a super-project manager. They may design a work flow that is optimal in some cases, but it is bound to be inappropriate in others. Meanwhile, the flexibility of their organizations suffers.

By contrast, a leader focuses on the "meta-processes" by which everybody forms teams across organizational boundaries and every-body determines the appropriate project-management processes. These meta-processes ensure that people throughout the organization assemble just the right people at just the right time to make just the right contributions. Meta-processes also let each team tailor its work flow to fit the project's unique needs, and ensure that each team member has clear accountabilities.

In summary, managers focus on results, and do so day after day. Leaders focus on the organizational processes that enable everybody to produce results forevermore. Working at the leadership level leverages executives' time, and reduces the risk of executive bottlenecks.

8. Organizational Engineers

Let's say you're committed to being a leader and building a healthy organization — one in which everybody can succeed. How can you improve relations with clients and reinvigorate and empower your staff, while keeping your organization under control? Or, put another way, how can you improve the health of your organization?

When problems become apparent, it's tempting to treat them in the most simple, direct manner. But this isn't always the right thing to do. Performance problems are often symptoms of dysfunctions built into the organizational environment.

For example, one leader was concerned about a lack of teamwork, and was about to hire a consultant to do some team-building — that is, conduct training programs that build interpersonal skills and relationships. But when he analyzed the problem more deeply, he found that teamwork was inhibited by a number of other deeper causes.

For one, people in different groups did not perceive the same priorities. When your highest priority is someone else's lowest, it'll be tough to get their help when you need it.

For another, he found that people were so focused on serving external clients that they broke commitments to each other the moment a client needed their help. Of course, if you can't trust your peers to keep their internal commitments to you, you'll do the work yourself rather than invite peers onto your team.

Typically, treating symptoms has little effect. In this case, team-building would have done little good. No matter how well people get along with one another, teamwork won't happen until they fix the way that internal priorities and commitments are managed.

Worse, treating symptoms can create other problems. For example, team-building could induce people to depend on each other more frequently. But until the problems with priorities and commitments are fixed, the more people team, the greater the risk of project delays.

Furthermore, treating symptoms is not lasting. Until root causes are addressed, problems will crop up again and again.

To fix problems once and for all, and to build high-performance organizations, leaders must introduce *systemic* change at the most fundamental root-cause level.

Systemic change is not just a matter of reengineering a few processes, or adding some new functions, or simply preaching the values of quality and customer focus. Executives must do more than make critical decisions, or lead the way on a few high-profile projects. They must fundamentally change the way the organization works.

A company's performance is the result of people's performance, which, in turn, is affected by the organizational environment they work in.

Consider how organizations affect people's performance: Organizations generate a system of influences that guides people in their decisions and actions. For example, the organizational environment defines the following:

*   Which stakeholders people represent, and whom they serve.

*   People's products, and the skills they should perfect.

*   Relationships among people, and the distribution of power.

*   Which behaviors are acceptable.

*   What work is funded.

*   How to get things done, and the tools and methods people use to do them.

*   Targets and measures of performance.

*   Which results are rewarded.

Just as road signs can either clearly direct you or lead you the wrong way, these organizational signals can either guide people toward high-performance teamwork or create chaos.

If an organization sends the right signals, people can be granted the freedom to make independent decisions with the assurance that they will automatically do the right things.

On the other hand, when an organizational environment sends the wrong signals, rational people behave irrationally. A clear and widespread example can be found in the many old-fashioned job-grading systems that base job level on the size of the group one manages (budget and headcount). This rewards people for maximizing expenses and growing empires, the opposite of the behaviors which organizations must foster to remain competitive.

When an organization sends the wrong signals, rational people behave irrationally.

Systemic change means adjusting the organizational drivers of everybody's behavior.

By building an organizational environment that sends the right signals, executives can impact a multitude of decisions, as if they were present at all times to gently guide everyone. If the signals are well coordinated, people can work in parallel on interrelated tasks and still produce an integrated set of products that are well aligned with business strategies, without executive intervention.

In this way, a healthy organization is the key to empowerment. In a well-designed organization, people can make decisions independently, and the signals throughout the organizational environment will guide them to make the right choices for the organization as a whole. This is a state of *organizational alignment*.

The best way to think about systemic change is to view organizations as complex machines, like automobiles. Like machines, organizations comprise a variety of systems (parts), each of which specializes in a certain function.

For example, in a car, the engine supplies motive power, the generator converts some of the power to electricity, the brakes slow the wheels, the suspension keeps the tires firmly planted on the road, the heater and air conditioner regulate cabin temperature, and the clock keeps time.

Within organizations, different systems guide people in resource management, job content, project selection and delivery, research and development, etc. These systems in organizations do not occur in sequence, first defining jobs, then setting priorities, then introducing methods, and finally measuring results. All these influences occur simultaneously, all the time.

And to make things even more complex, all an organization's systems must be interlinked. In a car, the fuel system continually feeds the engine just the right amount of gas, the valves let fuel in and exhaust out at just the right time, and the ignition system sparks the fuel at exactly the right instant.

Similarly, within an organization, all the systems that generate signals must be coordinated and attuned to both the organization's business strategies and the clients' needs. This coordination must occur within small groups, within project teams, and across the entire organization. For example, it does no good to recognize people for innovation when their job is to manage a stable infrastructure.

In summary, organizations (like automobiles) are made up of a wide variety of specialized systems, all operating in parallel, and yet interlinked. For organizations to survive, every system in them must send people the right signals, and all must be well coordinated. This is a "dynamic systems" view of organizations.

The systems within organizations are quite mechanistic. They send signals based on well-defined policies, rules, processes, and metrics.

Let's be perfectly clear about this: *People* are not machines and cannot be redesigned. But executives can design organizations that send people the right signals. Once they do so, they can feel comfortable that empowered people will independently apply their creativity and capabilities to each situation without any loss of organizational coordination and control.

An organization is well aligned when it sends signals that guide people to independently make the right decisions for the organization as a whole.

With this in mind, we can expand on our definition of "leadership." Leaders design the organizational systems that influence everybody in every aspect of their work. By doing so, they improve either the performance of a function or the coordination of the various functions within an organization.

Leader are akin to *organizational engineers* who, through precise and carefully planned changes in the design of the organization, repair, improve, and better interlink its many parallel systems. While a manager may be seen as a cog in the machine, a leader is the designer of the machine.

Leadership is not a matter of defining a business planning process that gets people to think through the critical issues of the day. Rather, leadership is a way of ensuring that a diverse set of ongoing processes is working well, and that people throughout the organization are well coordinated. Then, everybody can work through their subset of the critical issues in response to an ever-changing business environment, day after day.

A leader is not a cog in the machine, but rather a designer of the machine.

Executives at every level spend part of their time dealing with day-to-day management issues (as cogs in the machine). And management issues (such as strategies) can be extremely important.

But in addition, executives are responsible for leadership. It is their job to ensure a healthy organizational environment for themselves and everybody else.

ORGANIZATIONAL

DESIGN

*Take care of the means, and
the end will take care of itself.*

— Mohandas Gandhi —

9. The Systems Within Organizations

If organizations are like machines, then leaders must become "organizational engineers" who skillfully design the machines.

Just as science is applied in the field of engineering, science can also be applied in the design of organizations. A *systematic leader* is one who works *scientifically* on the fundamental organizational systems that guide people in their day-to-day work.

Systematic leaders improve
the way organizations operate
by applying science to the design of
the organizational systems
that guide people in their day-to-day work.

Oddly enough, many executives know how to design a business strategy (as a cog in the machine), but few know how to engineer a healthy organization. Nonetheless, this is the key to every leader's success.

The science of organizational design is a core competence of leadership.

To begin to define the science of organizational design, consider the question: What can an executive redesign without slipping into the day-to-day activities that lack leverage — that is, without becoming a cog in the machine?

Not every executive-level issue is an aspect of organizational design. Organizational systems have three qualities:

* They are stable.
* They are pervasive, and influence everyone's performance.
* They are controllable, and can be consciously designed.

Organizational systems are stable, influence everyone's performance, and can be consciously designed.

Stable

Organizational systems do not change quickly. If they did, people would experience constant chaos as their organizations are repeatedly redesigned. Instead, organizations need to be engineered to adapt to the changes around them without requiring fundamental changes in their design.

For example, goals and strategies are certainly of great interest to executives. But they are not organizational systems because they are not stable. They must adapt quickly to a changing environment.

When executives determine strategies, they are wearing their "management" hat, not their "leadership" hat. Leaders don't personally determine strategies. They don't have enough time to consider all the many strategic issues across every aspect of their organizations in the short time frames required by the volatile business environment. Instead, leaders design organizations that automatically formulate strategies — day after day, not once a year — to respond to new business threats and opportunities on a multitude of fronts.

Similarly, executives who work on clients' strategic problems are serving in the capacity of salespeople. They are doing one day-to-day function of the organization, not improving its effectiveness at all its functions. By contrast, the leader who introduces methods for identifying clients' strategic problems enables the whole organization to deliver strategic value day after day.

Leaders design organizations that automatically formulate strategies — day after day, not once a year — to respond to new business threats and opportunities on a multitude of fronts.

Pervasive

Organizational systems influence everybody, since their purpose is to allow widespread empowerment without loss of coordination or control. Those aspects of an executive's job that don't touch everybody in the organization lack leverage and are not systemic.

For example, executives' personal styles affect those with whom they interact, but not everybody in the organization. While a few may be inspired by a charismatic executive, the effect is neither pervasive nor lasting.

Furthermore, style is an outcome of the organizational environment, not a driving factor. People develop styles that succeed, and the definition of success is driven by the design of the organization. It does no good to teach people a new style (e.g., an entrepreneurial spirit that does the most with the least) when all the signals they get from the organization reinforce their old style (e.g., evaluating jobs based on the size of their budgets and headcount). By contrast, the leader who adjusts the organizational signals automatically influences everyone's style.

Hiring the right staff is also of great interest to executives, but it, too, is not an organizational system. Staffing decisions are an important ongoing supervisory duty, but they do not influence everybody in the organization; i.e., they are not systemic.

If an organization is not well designed, good people will appear to be poor performers. Firing them will only bring in a new batch of good people who will also perform poorly because of the unhealthy organizational environment around them.

Too often, people become the scapegoats of executives who, perhaps unwittingly, do not tackle the tough challenges of leadership. With the exception of obvious performance problems, replacing people should be a last resort, and not considered until after the organization is redesigned to bring out the best in everyone.

Controllable

Organizational systems must be within the control of executives or they are not worth discussing. Productive leaders remember the adage, "If you can't fix it, don't worry about it."

For example, human nature is stable and pervasive, but not something executives can design. Instead of treating it as an aspect of the organization, human nature is part of the "reality" in which organizations must succeed. Using sports as a metaphor, it is part of the playing field, not a leader's game-plan.

There are a number of things that, like human nature, are beyond the scope of leadership, including the national economy, laws and regulations determined by higher powers, and the behavior of people outside of the organization (such as clients).

The Five Organizational Systems

There are five systems within every organization which meet these three criteria: they are relatively stable; they influence everyone's performance; and they can be consciously (or unconsciously) designed by an executive. The five systems are: culture, structure, the internal economy, methods and tools, and metrics and rewards. (See Figure 2.)

The five organizational systems don't need to change day-by-day as the world changes. Rather, they define a set of processes that allow an organization to adapt dynamically to new challenges without having to rethink the way people work.

The next five chapters examine each of these five systems in turn. Each chapter defines the system and the subsystems within it, lists the symptoms that might trace their root cause to the system, and describes what it takes to implement changes in that system.

Leadership versus Management

Figure 1

LEADERSHIP	MANAGEMENT
Establish clear performance objectives for the organization	Formulate day-to-day strategies; plan and implement tactics
Communicate a vision of the way the organization should operate	Generate ideas; get venture capital; make operational decisions
Drive organizational transformations	Manage resources and people (performance management)
Represent the organization to stakeholders (e.g., to executives)	Represent the organization to its customers
Model and coach the attributes of leadership and entrepreneurship	Model and coach the attributes of the profession

The Systems
Within Organizations

Figure 2

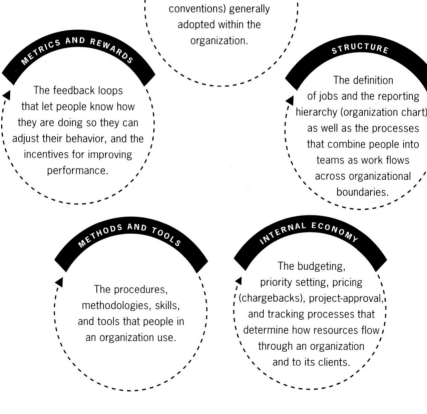

CULTURE
The behavioral patterns (habits and conventions) generally adopted within the organization.

METRICS AND REWARDS
The feedback loops that let people know how they are doing so they can adjust their behavior, and the incentives for improving performance.

STRUCTURE
The definition of jobs and the reporting hierarchy (organization chart), as well as the processes that combine people into teams as work flows across organizational boundaries.

METHODS AND TOOLS
The procedures, methodologies, skills, and tools that people in an organization use.

INTERNAL ECONOMY
The budgeting, priority setting, pricing (chargebacks), project-approval, and tracking processes that determine how resources flow through an organization and to its clients.

The RoadMap
Planning Process

Figure 3

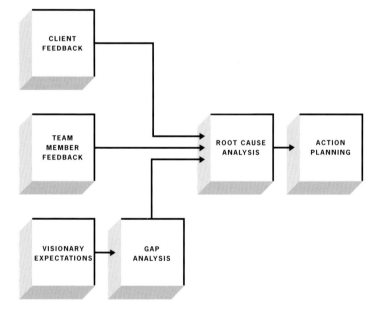

Example of a RoadMap

Figure 4

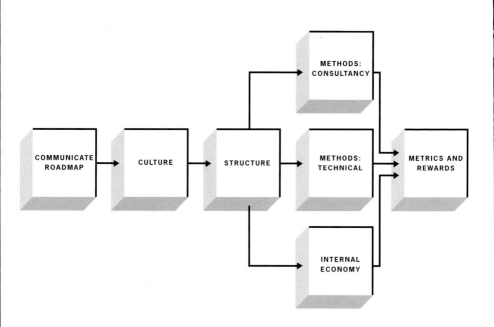

10. Culture

Culture may be broadly defined to include all the beliefs, values, attitudes, rituals, and behavior patterns that people in an organization share.

Despite the interest in values as a lever of leadership, people's beliefs, values, and attitudes are extremely difficult to change directly. And meddling with them verges on dubious ethics. Similarly, trying to tell people how to feel is futile.

On the other hand, specific behaviors can be described, modeled, and taught. Practical leaders focus on the *practices* that are widely accepted throughout their organizations. In this light, culture is "the way we work around here."

Culture is the set of behaviors that are widely practiced throughout an organization.

For example, telling people to trust one another (a feeling) is not likely to have any significant impact. Nor is the statement, "We value trust." But demanding that "we make no commitments that we cannot keep" (a behavior) ensures that people act in a trustworthy manner.

Once behaviors change, values and attitudes generally follow. In this example, once people behave in a trustworthy manner, they will learn to trust one another.

Culture applies to everyone in an organization. It does not include profession-specific practices. For example, a culture of customer focus should be widespread. But the specific practice of working with clients to identify their needs is limited to one profession within an organization (the "Consultancy," or sales force), and is, therefore, outside the scope of culture.

One of the major challenges facing many organizations is to convert a bureaucratic culture into an entrepreneurial culture. In a bureaucracy, people are given a set of resources and manage them as best they can. They think in terms of following procedures and performing tasks. Bureaucrats get ahead by building empires.

In an entrepreneurial culture, the opposite is true. Entrepreneurs run lines of business, and find ways to serve their customers by acquiring whatever resources are needed. They focus on delivering products (i.e., results), and are empowered to perform any tasks and utilize any processes needed to get the job done. Entrepreneurs abhor overhead (the bureaucrat's empire), and always try to do the most with the least.

Entrepreneurship means continually thinking about what it takes to keep your group competitive and your customers satisfied, and behaving with the same initiative and caring as if the business were your own.

By the way, moving to an entrepreneurial culture does not mean eliminating the "safety net" that attracted people to work for large organizations in the first place. It does not mean putting your personal assets or income at risk, or losing your job the minute business turns down.

Entrepreneurship means continually thinking about what it takes to keep your group competitive and your customers happy, and behaving with the same initiative and caring as if the business were your own. (Note that this presumes an ethical company that cares about its people.)

While you can't demand that people care about the business, the specific behaviors of entrepreneurs can be described as part of an organizational culture. For example, leaders might say, "We proactively seek new opportunities to better serve our customers by improving existing products and developing our capability to deliver new products." And by adopting new behaviors, people naturally learn to see their jobs in a new light.

In thinking about cultural change, leaders should focus only on their own organization, not on their clients'. The clients' culture is beyond their direct control. However, when people within an organization change the way they deal with others, then clients naturally begin to treat them differently. For example, when people pursue clear contracts with clients before starting work on projects, clients quickly learn to appreciate the value of such mutual understandings and reinforce this businesslike practice.

The culture of an internal service function does not have to match the broader culture of the company. Of course, people must obey the company's rules of conduct and relate to clients in the clients' language and style. Within those broad constraints, a service department can maintain a different internal culture. Indeed, most companies comprise a variety of cultures, each tailored to the needs of its various groups.

This clearly defined scope, combined with an emphasis on tangible behaviors within the organization, makes culture a powerful and practical tool of leadership.

Subsystems

Entrepreneurship is just one of many themes within the broad subject of culture. Commonly discussed themes include the following:

* Ethics (right versus wrong).
* Integrity (inspiring trust).
* Interpersonal relations (how we treat each other).
* Meetings (scheduled business events).
* Cooperation among peers (as one organization).
* Teamwork on projects.
* Empowerment (matching authority to accountability).
* Customer focus.
* Entrepreneurship (remaining competitive).
* Contracts (making commitments).
* Quality (fulfilling commitments).
* Risk.

Symptoms

Common practices that are not in the best interests of an organization, its staff, or its clients indicate the need for cultural change.

Innovation: For example, in Pat's case (described in Chapter 1), people may not think about keeping their product lines up to date, so the pace of innovation slows.

Customer focus: Pat's staff may think they know what's best for their customers, and as a result they may attempt to dictate clients' decisions or control them, which is the opposite of customer focus.

Strategic alignment: Strategic alignment suffers if staff make clients' decisions for them, because staff can never understand clients' businesses as well as their clients do.

Client relationships: Pat's clients and staff may be upset about frequent misunderstandings because the culture doesn't support contracting, that is, forming clear mutual agreements at the beginning of every project.

Project delivery: Culture can also affect project delivery. Contracts may be neglected once a project begins, leading to ever-increasing requirements ("scope creep"). Or Pat's people may be more comfortable saying "yes" to clients' demands (even if they know they cannot deliver) rather than an honest, "No, but here's what I *can* do for you."

By making unrealistic commitments, people take on more work than they can handle. And, as they try to juggle their commitments, projects slip and disappointed clients learn that they cannot trust the organization.

Costs: Culture may induce high costs if people always try to maximize quality rather than allow their customers to specify the required level of quality.

Empowerment: The culture may not support empowerment if people who give assignments request tasks rather than deliverables, or if people who receive assignments don't negotiate all the resources and authorities they need to succeed.

Teamwork: Teamwork suffers if the culture doesn't encourage people to behave in a reliable manner, forcing others to strive to be self-sufficient. For example, people may breach internal contracts (agreements) if a seemingly more important client requests their help. People must trust their peers within the organization before they're willing to form teams, and trust depends on respecting commitments to each other as much as commitments to clients.

Another common cultural problem related to teamwork occurs when people make promises to their customers before they check with their team members (their internal suppliers). Later, when they realize their internal suppliers are not available, they're forced to do the work themselves. In addition, people must agree to work through each other, rather than step on others' territories or hire their external competitors.

Other cultural principles can guide people to keep one another informed, promote other's interests, and work well together.

In general, whenever people throughout an organization (as opposed to just those in particular functions) don't demonstrate the right intuition or exhibit unproductive behaviors, culture may very well be the root cause.

Solutions

Cultural change begins with carefully crafted principles of behavior, written in such a way that everybody knows exactly what to do. The various principles can be grouped into sub-topics (chapters), and published in a document that is distributed throughout an organization.

Of course, just announcing new practices is not enough. Publishing a document, hanging up posters, and distributing coffee mugs with a few catchy sayings printed on them has little impact. Turning words into actions requires that everybody really understand the intended behaviors and can apply them to their daily work.

Education is best done in small-group sessions in which people have time to ask questions and fully understand each principle. In these sessions, it helps to translate principles into local practices by discussing what people in the group must do differently. These sessions can also be used to gather people's feedback and update the principles accordingly.

Education must be reinforced by continued leadership modeling and mentoring, and by incorporating adoption of the new culture into people's performance appraisals.

11. Structure

Structure defines people's jobs and specialties, as well as their relationships with one another. It determines who does what, and how people collaborate to get work done.

Structure includes the organization chart that defines people's jobs, and the work flows that combine people onto teams to produce the organization's products and services.

Structure is an extremely powerful organizational system. It determines people's knowledge and skills by focusing them on a specialty, and it gives them a sense of value by defining what piece of the business they run. It defines people's work products, i.e., their product lines, and determines who does what. It also determines people's biases by defining the topics they study and the stakeholders they represent.

Structure is a strong motivator since it is the basis for people's missions, charters, performance measures, and rewards.

Structure also influences everybody's relationships with one another, since job descriptions define who serves whom by determining products produced for internal customers.

In fact, structure is generally the most powerful organizational system.

Subsystems

Structure includes two major subsystems that are tightly intertwined:

*   The *organization chart* that defines people's specialties (i.e., lines of business).

*   The *work flows* that cross boundaries within an organization (i.e., the way the various specialists are combined to form multi-disciplinary project teams).

The *organization chart* divides the total mission of an organization among groups, hopefully without gaps or overlaps. The basis by which groups are divided tells people what they're supposed to be good at; i.e., it determines their specialty.

For example, if groups are divided by client (business unit, industry, or market segment), they will get to know their clients very well and become generalists with regard to other dimensions (such as the organization's products and technologies). On the other hand, if groups are divided by technologies, they will become specialists in their respective disciplines and gain only a general knowledge of clients' businesses. In a healthy organization chart, boundaries are defined in terms that match people's specialties.

Furthermore, in a healthy structure, groups are defined by product lines (i.e., what they produce for clients and each other) rather than by tasks or "roles and responsibilities" (what they do). The result is termed "whole jobs," where people are responsible for every aspect of producing a set of products or services.

With whole jobs, people can be entrepreneurial, and they feel a sense of ownership of a portion of their organization's business.

Whole jobs are also the basis for empowerment. By focusing them on products and services, people become creative about the processes by which they deliver those results. Furthermore, whole jobs are the basis for customer focus, since people who "sell" products understand they have customers to please.

Work flows are an equally integral part of structure. If people cannot depend on one another, they must become self-sufficient. Then, no matter what their organization chart looks like, its boundaries will not be respected. People will naturally evolve into small islands of generalists who replicate all the skills necessary to satisfy their customers.

In fact, those who give up on improving the processes of cross-boundary teamwork intentionally design "stovepipe" organizations made of little groups of generalists who do everything for a given business process (a common result of business process reengineering). Of course, these generalists cannot compete with better-designed organizations of specialists.

On the other hand, the better people are at teaming across organizational boundaries, the more they can focus on their respective specialties and the better they will perform.

In the past, many organizations depended on the management hierarchy to form and coordinate project teams. Of course, this creates bottlenecks that reduce an organization's capabilities. A healthy organizational structure includes mechanisms that induce self-forming and self-managing teams.

The most flexible approach to work flows is to think of each group as an independent business within a business, selling products and services to peers within the organization as well as to clients. Each project is assigned to the group that sells that product. This "prime contractor" then forms a project team by "hiring" subcontractors from throughout the organization.

In this way, teams quickly form across boundaries without the need for management intervention. Teams include just the right people at just the right time. And accountabilities are always clear, so people on the project team can be trusted to deliver their share of the project.

(Note that this doesn't mean that money changes hands. Rather, it's a powerful paradigm of project planning.)

To make this process work, the design of structure must include the definition of every group's product line. Inherent in these definitions of products, people sort out who sells what to whom, and the patterns of teamwork are established.

In summary, structure must consider both the organization chart that defines everyone's lines of business (people's specialties), and the processes of teamwork that cross organizational boundaries.

Symptoms

Because its impacts are so potent, structure is at the root of many common performance problems.

Innovation: In Pat's case, the organization chart may be the cause of their lack of innovation. If any group responsible for innovation reports to a manager responsible for operations, new ideas will be blocked by a boss whose job it is to keep things stable.

Or people may not be allowed to innovate if all the responsibility for thinking about the future is assigned to an "emerging technologies," "R&D," or "planning" group. This wastes many bright minds while creating a bottleneck for innovation.

Strategic alignment: The organization chart could also explain Pat's lack of strategic alignment and customer focus. If an organization lacks a separate "Consultancy" or sales group (a common problem in internal service organizations), no one will have the full-time job of getting to know clients and representing their interests. As a result, clients are likely to feel neglected.

Worse, no one will be independent of the organization's specific product lines and capable of analyzing clients' needs without bias. People who manage specific product lines will naturally recommend what they know, which may or may not be the most strategic product the organization has to offer.

Client relationships: Without a Consultancy, no one will be in a position to mediate agreements with clients without vested interests. If contracts are less clear, disputes will be more painful.

Empowerment and motivation: The organization chart can dis-empower and demotivate people. When jobs are defined by tasks rather than product lines, then jobs are not "whole" (i.e., they may not include total accountability for and authority over deliverables). People without product lines cannot identify with customers, won't feel a sense of ownership of a piece of their organization's business, and cannot be empowered. They are demotivated by the feeling that the organization expects them to simply do as they're told and doesn't really respect their creative ideas.

Pat's people may also be discouraged and demotivated if career paths are fragmented, or if the organization chart creates two "classes of citizenship." For example, when the structure separates a development group (that does the fun projects) from a maintenance group (that only does relatively mundane work), the people in the maintenance group contribute less, feel less valuable, and their career opportunities might be limited.

Project delivery: Structure could be the cause of Pat's unreliable project delivery. Both the organization chart and work-flow problems can destroy teamwork. If people can't get help from peers, they must become self-sufficient generalists who are "jacks of all trades, but masters of none."

Of course, the organization chart may quite intentionally create stovepipes if it divides people into groups based on anything other than their specialties. For example, designating a group of engineers, or "Technologists," for each client business unit (as in a decentralized function) creates small groups of generalists that cannot spend enough time on any one topic to master it.

Whatever the reason people must become self-sufficient, the result is the same: generalists cannot perform as well as teams of specialists with well-focused jobs. This adds up to people who are less capable of getting projects done, and projects will be delayed.

Innovation: Since generalists cannot keep up with the literature of their profession as well as specialists, the pace of innovation slows.

Costs: Parallel groups of generalists must each study the same skills and research the same products and methods. These multiple learning curves are expensive. A great deal of costly replication of effort is inevitable, and the results are fragmented and costly to maintain. And, of course, generalists cannot perform as efficiently or produce as high a quality as specialists, further increasing costs.

Symptoms of structural dysfunctions can be sorted by the two subsystems: the organization chart, and work flows.

Symptoms of dysfunctions in the *organization chart* include:

* Unclear boundaries, i.e., confusion about roles and responsibilities (and potential territorial disputes).

* Confusion about where to go for what.

* Redundant efforts.

* Lack of focus and burn-out.

* Poor quality or lack of professionalism due to lack of specialization.

* Unclear career paths.

* Unreliable processes and critical functions that don't occur without executive intervention because no one is looking after them.

* Inappropriate biases and potential conflicts of interests when jobs combine operational and innovation duties, or when product specialists serve as client liaisons.

* Lack of empowerment, or people who do no more than do as their told, when jobs are defined in terms of tasks rather than lines of business.

* Lack of sharing and cooperation due to territorial friction among similar professionals.

* Lack of product-line integration because no one is looking after design standards.

* Inefficiencies due to lack of internal support services.

The organization chart may clearly define where people should go for help; but if the work flows are dysfunctional, people may not get the help they need. Symptoms showing the need for improvement in *work flows* include:

* Lack of recognition of people's interdependence, and the resulting lack of cooperation.

* Difficulty getting the right people on project teams at the right time.

* Chronic confusion about accountabilities and control within project teams.

* Replication of others' skills to avoid interdependence (perhaps with territorial disputes, redundant efforts, etc.).

* An "assembly-line" mentality that isn't flexible in the way that people are selected for project teams.

* Unclear contracts (agreements) with clients, since people are unclear about their product lines.

* People making clients' decisions or doing clients' jobs for them due to lack of clear agreements about their respective accountabilities.

Solutions

Because of the tight relationship between the organization chart and work flows, a well-planned restructuring treats both subsystems together.

Effective structural change begins with a leadership team that studies the science of organizational structure, agrees on a common language to describe the building blocks of structure, and applies a common set of principles to designing a new structure.

A "clean sheet of paper" approach to the organization chart is recommended. Small adjustments to an extant organization chart actually take longer and are much more painful (emotionally and politically), since people naturally try to protect their territories. Furthermore, a series of small changes keeps people in chaos, with continued uncertainty and fear. This is far more difficult for staff than one big change.

Once the organization chart is determined, work flows are developed. To build the basis for high-performance teamwork, each group drafts its own "charter" — a list of the products and services it sells to each of its customers (clients and peers), and those it buys from each of its suppliers. This is combined with a discipline of subcontracting to peers for specific products (rather than simply drafting people onto teams).

Charters then become the basis for "walk-throughs" — practice in how real work will be done by documenting work flows as a series of contracts and subcontracts.

With enough preparation, the new structure can be highly productive shortly after it is announced. More importantly, by planning the work flows as well as the organization chart, the new structure will not simply be a matter of "rearranging the deck chairs on the Titanic." Instead, it will bring about significant changes in the way that people work.

12. Internal Economy

The internal economy encompasses all the processes related to the management of money and time. It includes the various resource-allocation and investment-decision processes within an organization that determine how much of each product line to make, what specific products and services are produced, and who gets them.

The internal economy includes all the resource-management processes that determine how much of each product line to make, what specific products and services are produced, and who gets them.

These resource-management processes are often viewed as accounting systems. However, accounting only reports past events. Viewing these same processes as an *economy* reveals how decisions about the future are made.

For companies, it's clear that clients (outside the firm) make purchase decisions and pay for the products and services they receive. For internal service departments, clients within the company may or may not be charged for the products and services they "buy."

Internal "chargebacks," i.e., charging a price for products and services, are an important aspect of the internal economy (although only relevant in the most advanced evolutionary stages of an internal economy). But the internal economy includes far more than pricing and cost accounting. It also encompasses clients' investment decision processes (budgeting) and their ability to make effective purchase (priority) decisions; providers' investment decision processes and their ability to run effective entrepreneurships; and the accounting mechanisms by which resources flow through an organization and people get the information they need.

Whether or not an organization charges clients for its products, what happens to the money thereafter, as it flows through the organization, is a significant issue. These resource flows affect how priorities are set and how investment decisions are made for the various groups within the organization.

There are a variety of evolutionary stages of the internal economy, ranging from the relatively simple but least effective "Centrally Planned" economy to a free market.

Many internal service organizations currently live in a "Centrally Planned" economy where there are no internal chargebacks. Instead, a budget is given directly to the service provider (rather than its customers). Much of that budget may go to routine operations and overhead. But for the portion available for client-driven projects, a steering committee (a central "soviet"), a "czar," or worse, the individual provider groups, manages the available hours and decides what projects will be done.

This primitive form of internal economy can be made to work, although it is far from ideal. In a healthy Centrally Planned economy, the organization treats its budget as a "prepayment" for the products and services it will provide in the year ahead. Client representatives (typically a steering committee) make decisions about priorities, and the organization does no work without their "funding" it from the prepaid account.

In the next evolutionary stage, a "Labor Shadow Market" economy, individual client business units are given shares of an organization's available project hours. Each business unit can spend its hours on any projects it pleases, giving it control over priorities within its share of the total available resources. Of course, only the hour-based products (people's time) are under the clients' control; the rest of the organization's budget is still managed by the organization itself.

The more advanced "Monetary Shadow Market" allocates money rather than hours to business units, and then charges the costs of products and services to these allocations. (I.e., invoices are paid with what is sometimes called "funny money".) This gives clients control over both people's time and other products such as operational services and capital goods. But it does require the development of a price list that attaches a fair share of total costs to each of an organization's many products.

The most advanced form of internal economy, Fee for Service, is a true market where clients receive the budget for a function rather than the service department that provides the function. Internal entrepreneurs charge real money (true "chargebacks," either at cost or market rates), and earn revenues to cover their expenses by selling their products and services. Some limited budget is still given directly to service departments for subsidies for "corporate-good" activities and for "equity" to develop new business ventures. This empowers both clients to control their factors of production by deciding what they will and won't buy, and service providers to invest in their businesses.

Each more advanced stage brings additional benefits, but is also significantly more complex. Moving ahead through the stages requires not only careful planning, but also significant learning by both clients, who are increasingly in control of resource-investment decisions, and by internal entrepreneurs, who are increasingly subject to competitive pressures.

When it comes to implementing an effective internal economy, "the devil's in the details."

Subsystems

There are four subsystems within the internal economy:

* **Spending power:** the allocation of resources, i.e., budgeting, that determines who controls what spending power and earmarks resources for overhead and reinvestment in the organization's business. This subsystem fills up "checkbooks" for clients and internal projects, and turns those checkbooks over to "pursers." It is critical to strategic alignment, and to the organization's ability to reinvest in itself in order to remain viable in the future.

* **Purchase decisions:** the priority-setting process that allocates spending power to projects and ongoing services, giving pursers control over their purchases. It determines who can "sign checks." This subsystem is a critical ingredient in balancing supply and demand, and in determining return on investments.

* **Pricing:** the costs allocated to each product, and the prices charged for them. This subsystem also determines the funding of activities that should not be charged to clients but rather are part of overhead, such as training, product development, and working with clients on new business opportunities. When budgets are given directly to internal service providers, pricing is inherent in the services that are expected for a given level of budget. Of course, in a Fee-for-Service economy, pricing determines chargebacks.

* **Tracking:** the reporting that gives pursers the information they need to manage their spending power (telling them what's left in their checkbooks and where their money went), and entrepreneurs the information they need to manage their businesses.

Symptoms

Innovation: The internal economy may be one of the causes of a lack of innovation. In Pat's case, demand clearly exceeds supply. People may be so busy trying to please clients that they can't take the time to keep themselves up to date. As a result, innovation slows.

The internal economy also determines what overhead is imbedded within prices (or internal budgets). If the budget doesn't include a reserve for applied research and product development, innovation won't be funded. Or if prices are set such that people must work on client-oriented projects for too high a percentage of their time just to break even, they will not have sufficient "unsold" time to evolve their skills and products. In either case, innovation suffers.

Sometimes, new business ventures are needed to diversify the product line. If the internal economy does not provide a source of "venture capital," significant innovations will not be funded.

Strategic alignment: For internal service organizations, strategic alignment will suffer if providers set their own priorities rather than insisting that clients decide what they'll buy, because staff can never understand clients' businesses as well as the line managers who run them.

Another potential problem is that strategic investments may be blocked if it takes too long to get projects past various layers of approvals. By the time the priority-setting process gets around to considering an investment, the window of opportunity may be gone.

Customer focus: Pat's people may not be customer focused if they don't reserve sufficient "overhead" time for working with customers on new business (a problem in the pricing subsystem).

In internal service functions, customer focus suffers further when the budget is supplied by the boss rather than earned by serving clients. People will naturally try to please the boss who funds them rather than clients. This may appear as a culture in which staff look after the company's interests rather than serve individual clients (i.e., where people think they know what's best for their clients and act as an audit function, the antithesis of customer focus).

Decentralization: Of course, if an internal service department sets its own priorities rather than allowing clients to determine what they'll buy, clients will resent losing control of one of their factors of production. This explains one threat Pat faces, and is a common cause of pressure for decentralization.

Responsiveness: If demand exceeds supply and people are overworked, Pat's staff may appear unresponsive to their clients, no matter how hard they work.

A lack of responsive may also result from a project-approval process that is infrequent or convoluted. In extreme cases, organizations decide project priorities as part of an annual planning process, and find it very difficult to respond to new opportunities during the year.

Costs: The internal economy also has a significant impact on costs. For example, centralized budgeting guarantees an internal service function "market share," instead of subjecting it to competitive pressures that keep costs low. An organization in this situation won't automatically think about cost control, except perhaps once a year at budget time.

Or Pat's prices may include costs of "corporate good" activities that should be subsidized directly by the company.

Project delivery: Pat's concern for unreliable project delivery may be partially caused by the lack of teamwork that occurs when one group's highest priority is another's lowest. Priorities should be set (by clients) for the entire organization, not separately for each group within the organization.

A weak purser function may allow clients to ask for more and more ("scope creep"), whether they can afford it or not. This is another reason why delivery of projects may be uncertain.

The numerous indications of the need for process improvements in the internal economy can be sorted by the four basic subsystems: spending power, purchase decisions, pricing, and tracking.

In the *spending-power* (budgeting) subsystem, the following symptoms may occur:

* Too little budget, leading to an inability to pursue high-payoff projects and loss of strategic alignment.

* Too much budget, leading to expenditures on low-payoff work and loss of strategic alignment.

* An inappropriate allocation of spending power, where one client has too little and forgoes great investment opportunities while another has too much and wastes resources on low-payoff projects.

* Clients who lack an understanding of where their money is going, feel out of control, and desire decentralization.

* Prices that appear to be too high because they must cover the costs of "corporate good" activities (subsidies) that competitors don't have to do.

* Inadequate time and money for research, professional development, and other investments in the future viability of the organization.

* Difficulty expanding the product line for lack of venture capital.

The *purchase-decision* (priority-setting) process needs attention if the following symptoms are evident:

*   Demand far in excess of supply (backlogs), leading to people who are chronically overworked and an organization that appears unresponsive.

*   Clients who resent the organization for deciding on their behalf what they'll buy.

*   An infrequent priority-decision process (e.g., where project priorities are set only once a year in the budget process), leading to the inability to respond quickly to shifts in business strategy.

*   Poor investment decisions (i.e., poor strategic alignment) resulting from the wrong people deciding priorities or from pursers who lack adequate information.

*   Difficulty trusting teamwork, since one group's highest priority may be another's lowest, or where contracts with peers are not respected as much as contracts with clients.

Pricing might be the root cause if the following symptoms are observed:

*   Providers who do not have sufficient "overhead" funds or time to reinvest in keeping their businesses viable (e.g., in research and professional development), leading to a lack of innovation.

*   No incentives to customers for off-peak usage (load leveling), leading to high costs.

*   Customers vying for the "best" people to work on their projects for lack of differential pricing.

*   Clients who complain about high costs due to some products cross-subsidizing other under-priced products.

The *tracking* subsystem might be problematic if the following symptoms occur:

*   Providers who are not cost conscious.

*   Clients who don't know the limits of their spending power and expect more than an organization can deliver.

*   Excessive time spent analyzing costs.

Solutions

Fixing a dysfunctional internal economy requires a study team that includes both people within the organization and, in the case of internal service departments, representatives of its clients. Unlike the other organizational systems, changes to the internal economy require significant involvement by an organization's clients. Their decision processes are as important as those within the organization, and their power and well-being are directly affected by the internal economy.

The study team begins with education in the application of economics within the firm.

Then, it charts the "as is" state, and develops a detailed schematic that portrays how resources are managed and decisions are made.

The schematic is then scrutinized for dysfunctions, using a comprehensive list of analytic questions drawn from economic theory. If the organization charges fees for its products and services, the pricing matrix is also examined to identify inappropriate allocations of costs.

The next step is to select a target stage of evolution. An organization cannot go directly from a Centrally Planned to a Fee-for-Service economy. There are too many mechanical details that need to be worked out first. And, more importantly, it takes time for clients to learn to be smart buyers and for providers to learn to be effective entrepreneurs.

Moving through the stages of evolution too quickly can create more problems than it solves. (As evidence, note the bread lines, price riots, bankruptcies, and starvation experienced when the former Soviet-bloc nations moved into a market economy virtually overnight.) Each organization must select a target stage that is realistically within its grasp.

Once the target stage is decided, the study team can narrow its focus to those dysfunctions which will be solved now, versus those which must await future evolutionary steps. This leads to a practical and detailed action plan to stabilize the current stage or move methodically to the next evolutionary stage.

A year or two later, the team can reconvene to develop another action plan that moves the organization carefully to the next stage of evolution.

13. Methods and Tools

Methods and tools give people the capabilities they need to do their jobs well. "Methods" includes skills and procedures. Tools reinforce methods and extend people's skills. Methods and tools may include professional education, skills training, and the adoption of new technologies.

Methods and tools are the skills, procedures, and tools that give people the capabilities to do their jobs well.

Documented methods and modern tools describe the professional practices of individuals and the processes within groups (as distinct from structural work flows that describe the processes between groups within the organization).

This is the system of organizational learning. Once methods are documented, they can be taught, replicated, and enhanced.

On the other hand, if methods are left to individuals' intuitions, the organization's performance is constrained by each person's innate talents. Without documented methods, it's difficult to train new people, and experienced people lack a medium to learn from one another. Even talented and knowledgeable people perform less well, since the results they gained intuitively one time may not be replicatable in another situation (i.e., processes become unreliable). And, when methods are not documented, it's tough to make improvements based on experience.

Subsystems

There are two major classes of methods and tools:

* **Generic:** those which are of widespread use throughout the organization.

   Examples of organizationwide methods include project management, time management, customer service, entrepreneurship, marketing, business management, market forecasting, business planning, proposal writing, contracting, teaming skills, meeting skills, and general writing and communicating skills.

* **Profession specific:** those which are utilized only by specific groups within the organization.

   Examples include client needs assessments (sales), client benefits measurement, planned change management, account management, market research, emerging technologies research, product development, standards planning, project estimation, manufacturing operations, customer support, and training. The list is at least as long as the variants of specialties in the organization.

Symptoms

Responsiveness: People in Pat's organization might be unresponsive to clients and unreliable in delivering projects if they lack a good method for project estimation. If they routinely underestimate the effort required, they will take on more work than they can deliver and then struggle to meet impossible commitments.

Project delivery: Lack of project management methods and tools may cause unreliable project delivery.

Strategic alignment: Strategic alignment will suffer if Pat's organization lacks a method to help clients find high-payoff projects. If so, it may revert to "order taking" rather than proactively helping clients discover new uses for its products.

If Pat's organization lacks a method for measuring the strategic benefits of its products, clients will find it difficult to justify these less-tangible investments, and Pat's strategic alignment will suffer.

Payoff will also suffer if the organization cannot estimate the life-cycle costs of owning a product, making it difficult for clients to calculate their return on investments and make sound purchase decisions.

Costs: Costs will rise if any of Pat's people are inefficient for lack of modern methods and tools.

Methods and tools need attention if any of the following symptoms are seen in a specific area of the organization:

* Poor performance.
* Unreliable results.
* Results not improving with experience.
* Difficulty with cross-training.

In general, if symptoms can be treated through a one-time investment in training or tools, the system of methods and tools is likely to be the root cause. If ongoing investments in training and tools are needed, the root cause will be found in other systems.

Solutions

Improvements may involve research in state-of-the-art methods and tools, acquisition of both methods and tools, and training.

The profession-specific methods require that there exists a group in the structure with a focus on that profession (with the time and incentive to learn the method).

14. Metrics and Rewards

Metrics and rewards are the "feedback loops" that allow people to monitor their own results and adjust their behaviors accordingly. A simple example is the thermostat that measures room temperature and adjusts heating and air conditioning systems to keep a room comfortable.

Metrics and rewards are the feedback loops that tell people how they are doing and reward them for relevant performance.

Metrics and rewards focus people's attention. Put simply, people do what they are rewarded to do, and avoid behaviors which cause them pain. If people are measured on efficiency, their productivity will rise. If they're measured on quality, they may slow down a bit but quality will improve.

Subsystems

The concept of feedback loops includes two fundamental subsystems:

*   Metrics that keep people informed about their own perform-
    ance against target levels of performance (benchmarks).
    Metrics occur at two levels:
    -   Organizationwide.
    -   Profession-specific.

*   Rewards that are tied to performance.

Metrics tell people how they are doing. They can be defined at two levels: organizationwide measures of everybody's collective performance, and profession-specific measures of the performance of individuals or small-groups.

Organizationwide metrics tell people how well the whole organization is performing, but don't guide individual behaviors. They can be used to build concern for the state of the organization and motivate a desire for change (if they raise concerns), as well as celebrate successes (if they show progress).

Profession-specific metrics are required to impact people's day-to-day performance.

Profession-specific metrics include, but are certainly not limited to, the annual performance appraisal process. In fact, annual reviews are one of the least valuable forms of metrics. Imagine the oversimplified case of a machine operator who reads a dial and controls a knob. When the dial indicates that the machine is drifting out of tolerance, he adjusts the knob. Now imagine that the dial is moved to the supervisor's office, and the supervisor tells the operator how he did at the end of each year. What are the odds of a quality product? Zero!

To have a meaningful impact on results, metrics must be delivered to the people doing the work (not their supervisors). Furthermore, people must get the feedback in time for them to adjust their behaviors. Direct and timely feedback loops, termed "in-process" metrics (as opposed to after-the-fact evaluations), are the most powerful form of metrics.

Metrics include both feedback on how things are going, and the targets against which to compare and judge those measures. If your supervisor tells you that your performance deserved a grade of 8, you cannot know if that's good or bad until you know whether that was 8 out of an expected 10 or out of 100. People must have standards against which to judge the metrics of their performance.

Thus, the metrics subsystem includes "benchmarks" of performance, i.e., target levels for metrics.

As popular as the concept is, benchmarking is not always healthy. There are two types of benchmarks: those which compare your processes to others' (best practices), and those which compare your outcomes (performance targets).

Benchmarking other organizations' processes or adopting their "best practices" is particularly dangerous. Other organizations' solutions to familiar symptoms may work well for them, but fail to address the root causes of *your* problems. Indeed, mimicking others can create as many problems as they solve if their behaviors don't fit into your environment.

For example, ISO-9000 (a widely accepted standard of quality) emphasizes well-documented processes rather than results. People may go through the motions, but following a well-documented procedure won't guarantee that they're doing the right thing. Indeed, if people are measured on how well they follow a procedure, they won't even bother to think about whether the procedure is worth following.

In general, process metrics (which measure how people do things rather than results) are unwise. They lead people to "go through the motions," whether or not those motions accomplish anything. And they disempower people, forcing them to do tasks as assigned rather than apply their knowledge and creativity to attaining the intended results.

Benchmarking outcomes is safer, but can still be problematic. Targets phrased in terms like "as good as others" may not be high enough, and certainly won't lead to thinking creatively about what's possible or to "leap-frogging" the competition.

Targets are best based on a vision of the ideal, and then revised upward (but never downward) through comparisons to others. In this light, external comparisons should be done very late in the planning process so they don't constrain people's vision to others' current levels of performance.

Rewards encourage people to care about the metrics. Rewards need not be limited to money; they include all the things people find rewarding, such as recognition and appreciation, career-growth opportunities, discretion and influence, and even something as simple as a preferred parking place.

(Note: While leaders should be creative about non-monetary rewards, training opportunities should not be viewed as rewards. Doing so implies that the default is no investment in people unless warranted by exceptional performance. This creates a "Catch 22": poor performers who wish to improve through training but cannot.)

The subsystem of rewards also includes the adverse impacts of poor performance, i.e., fair but firm performance management. If poor performers are tolerated, everybody else will feel demotivated, as if their own performance doesn't matter.

Rewards should focus on individual or small-group performance (based on profession-specific metrics), not on team performance. In a well-aligned organization, there should be no need for team-oriented rewards, since doing what's best for your own entrepreneurship automatically means doing what's best for your customers and building healthy partnerships with your suppliers.

In fact, it's dangerous to reward people for team performance if other feedback loops are telling people not to serve the team. This only masks a more fundamental lack of organizational alignment. If teamwork is a problem, the better approach is to fix these conflicting signals rather than treat the symptoms with team-oriented metrics and rewards.

Clearly, rewards must be tied directly to the metrics which are within people's direct control. And to have maximum impact, rewards should be delivered as quickly as possible after the desirable behaviors occur.

Symptoms

Innovation: Pat's organization may not be motivated to be innovative if its metrics focus exclusively on delivering current projects. Remember, thinking about the future inevitably takes time away from today's tasks.

Customer focus: Similarly, if people are measured by their efficiency and not by customer satisfaction, customer focus will suffer. These are examples of metrics that may be appropriate, but are not comprehensive.

Empowerment and motivation: Misplaced metrics can be demotivational. Pat's people complained of a lack of identity with the business. This may be the result of metrics that focus on means (tasks) rather than on ends (deliverables), which disempower people and discourage them from taking responsibility for their results.

Costs: Pat's organization may also be the victim of perverse rewards. For example, if job grades are based on the size of people's budgets and the headcount that they manage, they are rewarded for empire building and for maximizing costs, not minimizing them.

In general, *metrics* need attention if the following symptoms occur:

*   People are unclear about what is expected of them to succeed in their jobs (beyond confusion about specific projects).

*   People set their levels of aspiration too low.

*   People are unable or unwilling to flexibly adapt their behavior in time to affect outcomes.

*   People pursue one objective at the expense of others (sub-optimization).

Rewards need attention if people are demotivated because they feel that their performance doesn't matter — to the organization or to them personally.

Solutions

Since metrics drive performance, people tend to optimize the objectives which are measured and ignore other important accountabilities. Thus, it is much more important that metrics be *comprehensive* rather than precise.

The City of Sydney, Australia, offers a classic case example. Commuter trains were running late, making people late for work. To fix this, some years ago, they began to measure and reward drivers based on whether their trains arrived on time. As a result, trains got downtown on time, but they did it by passing up stops (leaving customers on the platform) if they were running late!

An example of a comprehensive metric is Economic Value Added (E.V.A.), an organization's operating profits less the cost of capital employed. [2] While primarily applied to business units, similar concepts can be used to measure internal service functions within organizations (particularly in more advanced internal economies).

Another comprehensive metric is market share. For internal service providers, this equates to clients' willingness to work with a group (even if they, in turn, use outside vendors) rather than buy directly from external vendors or do the work themselves.

When comprehensive, quantitative metrics are not available, it's better to use managerial judgment than sacrifice comprehensiveness by measuring only the things which can be quantified.

2.   Stewart, G. Bennett. *The Quest for Value.* New York, NY: HarperCollins. 1991.

For example, 360-degree performance reviews are very effective. Individual performance is measured by including customers' input. Teamwork is measured through suppliers' input. Supervisory skills are measured by including subordinates input in their boss' performance appraisal. And business results are measured by the supervisor's judgments.

To be meaningful, metrics must focus on the *specific results* expected of each group (rather than the means of attaining them). And, of course, they must be *understandable,* expressed in units that people can easily relate to their behaviors.

Metrics must be *delivered to the person being measured, in time for him or her to adjust performance* to improve the metric.

Tying rewards to metrics amplifies the power of the metrics. To be fair, rewards should be based on well-defined metrics. A new reward system should only be implemented after the metrics have been implemented, tested, understood, and stabilized.

Like metrics, rewards must be meaningful to those doing the work. More money is nice, but may not be a strong enough motivator for everyone. Intangible rewards (be they recognition, freedom, or time off) may be more meaningful to some people. In fact, a reward to one person (such as a challenging assignment) may be a punishment to another. Rewards are in the eyes of the receivers.

To ensure that metrics and rewards are appropriate and relevant, a well-designed metrics program involves each group in designing its own feedback loops.

To help them, a team that includes specialists in the organization's structure (which defines each group's deliverables), the mechanics of measurement (e.g., information systems), and reward systems (e.g., compensation) can be assembled. This team can consult with each group to help it define and implement a set of metrics and rewards tailored to its unique mission and people.

THE PATH
FORWARD

*If you don't know where you are going,
it doesn't matter what road you take.*

— Lewis Carroll —

15. Getting to Your Roots

To put all the pieces together and practice root-cause analysis, think back to Pat's predicament, described in Chapter 1. For each symptom that surfaced in her interviews with clients and staff, let's speculate about possible root causes — a practical exercise in systemic thinking.

Lack of strategic alignment.

* *Culture:* If people *think* they know what's best for clients and attempt to "do what's right for the company," they do not respect clients' knowledge of their businesses and strategic alignment suffers.

* *Structure:* If the organization lacks a Consultancy or sales function, no one has sufficient time to know the clients' businesses very well, understand their strategies, and identify high-payoff opportunities without any technical bias.

* *Internal economy:* In internal service functions, if priorities are set by the organization rather than its clients, strategic alignment suffers.

   Alignment also suffers if it takes a long time for clients to get a project approved.

* *Methods and tools:* The organization may lack a method for analyzing clients' strategies and identifying high-payoff opportunities, or one for measuring and justifying the value-added benefits of its products.

   Also, if they lack methods for estimating clients' life-cycle costs of ownership, clients may make poor investment decisions.

Overcommitted, leading to lack of responsiveness and people feeling overworked.

*   *Culture:* If people would rather say "yes" and fail than say an honest "no" to commitments they cannot keep, they take on more work than they can handle, and their responsiveness and reputations suffer.

*   *Internal economy:* If demand exceeds supply, people are overworked and appear unresponsive to clients no matter how hard they try to keep up.

*   *Methods and tools:* If people are not trained in a reliable method of project forecasting, they may underestimate projects and take on more work than they can handle.

Lack of customer focus, in part due to unclear agreements.

*   *Culture:* If people don't routinely establish clear mutual understandings (contracts) at the beginning of every project, misunderstandings during the project are likely.

*   *Structure:* If the organization lacks a Consultancy or sales group, no one has the full-time job of looking after clients' satisfaction.

    Also, if people's jobs are defined in terms of tasks rather than results, they do not have products to sell or customers on which to focus.

*   *Internal economy:* In an internal service function, if budget is supplied by the boss rather than by clients (via fees for services), people naturally please their boss, not their clients.

    The internal economy may also fail to reserve time to work with clients on new ideas, leading to the appearance of a lack of interest in helping clients with their business problems.

*   *Metrics and rewards:* If the organization does not measure customer satisfaction but does reward people for other metrics

(such as efficiency), people naturally neglect their customers and instead focus inwardly on the mechanics of their jobs.

Unreliable project delivery.

* *Culture:* If people do not routinely form clear contracts with clients, projects may grow over time ("scope creep"), making it impossible to guarantee delivery dates.

* *Structure:* If teams do not form across organizational boundaries effectively, people have difficulty getting the help they need and have trouble delivering complex projects (ones that require a variety of disciplines).

* *Internal economy:* If priorities are set independently for each group in the organization (rather than as a single set of priorities for each source of money), people have difficulty getting help from peers and struggle with projects that require teamwork.

  Also, if the "purser" (priority-setting) function is weak, people may be permitted to expand the scope of projects, whether or not they can afford additional resources. As a result, clients' expectations exceed the organization's ability to deliver.

* *Methods and tools:* If people are not trained in a reliable method of project forecasting, they may underestimate projects. In that case, even if they get the work done efficiently, they appear unreliable.

  Of course, another method that is critical to reliable delivery is project management.

High costs.

* *Culture:* If people try to maximize quality in every case rather than satisfy their customer's expectations of quality, everything they do is "gold plated" and costs are excessive.

* *Structure:* If engineers (Technologists) are divided into groups by anything other than their skills, they cannot specialize in their discipline or area of technology. As a result, many small groups of generalists reinvent rather than reuse past work, results become fragmented, and they all must invest the time to learn everything — all of which dramatically increase costs.

* *Internal economy:* If an internal service organization receives a central budget, it has a guaranteed share of the internal market and is not subject to the competitive pressures (or even comparisons) that keep costs down.

* *Methods and tools:* If people lack modern methods and tools, they take longer to do things and costs rise.

* *Metrics and rewards:* If people's job grades are based on the size of their budgets and headcount, they naturally build empires rather than do the most with the least.

Lack of innovation.

* *Culture:* People who act like bureaucrats rather than entrepreneurs don't think about earning market share and fail to keep their product lines up to date.

* *Structure:* People may be reluctant to bring forward new ideas if their boss is primarily concerned with running a stable operation (i.e., when innovation functions report to operations).

  The organization may include an "emerging technologies" group that is a bottleneck to innovation.

  Or the structure may divide people into small groups of generalists who cannot stay up to date as well as specialists.

* *Internal economy:* An organization cannot be sufficiently innovative if the internal economy does not set aside time and money for product development, or if it forces people to dedicate such a high percentage of their time to project delivery that they have no time to think about the future.

*   *Metrics and rewards:* If people are rewarded solely for project delivery, they may focus all their efforts on completing current projects, leaving no time to prepare for the future.

Clients feel out of control of priorities.

*   *Internal economy:* If priorities are set by the organization itself or by a central committee rather than by individual business units, then clients are not in control and are bound to resent it.

Lack of staff identity with their business, leading people to focus on tasks rather than results.

*   *Culture:* If people who give and receive assignments don't clearly negotiate the bounds of empowerment, authority may not match accountabilities and people may not have control over their own results.

*   *Structure:* If jobs are defined in terms of tasks rather than product lines, people are not accountable for the organization's business and products.

If people cannot see a career path that allows them to get ahead, they feel demotivated.

Also, if the structure creates winners and losers (fun jobs and boring jobs), the losers become disenfranchised.

*   *Metrics and rewards:* Metrics which focus on processes rather than deliverables tell people to perform tasks without thinking about their results.

Lack of teamwork across organizational boundaries.

*   *Culture:* Many cultural principles are necessary to ensure healthy teamwork. For one, to ensure that others can deliver their portion of the project, people must check with their team members before making commitments to their customers. The absence of such appropriate behaviors leads to a lack of mutual trust and avoidance of interdependence and teamwork.

* *Structure:* Teamwork also depends on a meta-process for forming teams across boundaries, i.e., the work-flows subsystem. People may not understand the products they sell to each other, or the process of subcontracting with peers.

* *Internal economy:* If priorities are set independently for each group in the organization (rather than as a single set of priorities for each source of money), people have difficulty getting help from peers, since one group's highest priority may be another's lowest.

No Silver Bullets

In Pat's case, as in most organizations, there are no "silver bullets" that will solve all an organization's problems. All five systems are at work in every organization all the time. And, they are all interrelated, i.e., each must work in concert with the others.

To be effective, a leader must consider all five systems, and develop a plan that treats organizational health holistically.

Therefore, to be effective, a leader must consider all five systems, not just one in isolation, and develop a plan that treats organizational health holistically.

A transformational action plan determines precisely which symptoms will be treated within each of the five systems by tracing their root causes, and then adjusts all the systems in a well-planned sequence of changes.

Finding the Right Root Causes

As leaders analyze symptoms, it is critically important to trace each issue to the *right* root causes, that is, to the right organizational systems. Treating a symptom by changing the wrong system creates more problems than it solves.

For example, in an international distributor of commodities, everybody is critically dependent on information — about producers, storage facilities, transporters, customers, and world financial markets. As a result, the corporate information systems (I.S.) department is quite visible and important to everyone.

Of course, nobody likes being dependent on something he or she cannot control. The more people understand the importance of I.S. to their business, they more they want to control the I.S. department's activities. In itself, clients' desire for control is good — it indicates that clients recognize the importance of the I.S. function.

But this company's I.S. department was not within their control. It received a budget and set its own priorities (with some client input). This forced clients to beg for attention. Resenting this, clients demanded *decentralization,* a structural change, because they knew that if they "owned" their own I.S. groups, they would have absolute control over priorities.

Consider an analogy. You demand absolute control over what you eat. Yet you share a grocery store with your entire community. You don't feel the need to own a grocery store to control what you eat, since you control your spending power. You buy what you want, and don't buy things that don't seem worthwhile to you.

You're able to do this because we live in a market economy (akin to the *internal economy* described in Chapter 12); and the grocery store is customer focused (the only *culture* that works in a market economy, as discussed in Chapter 10), and the store works hard to supply you with just what you want (and will pay for).

Note that if you did have to own your own grocery store (a decentralized *structure*), you'd find a much smaller selection on the shelves, experience more waste, and incur higher overhead (since fixed costs could not be shared with your neighbors). Meanwhile, you'd have to learn to personally manage purchasing, storage, and logistics — an unnecessary expense and a nuisance!

Translating this analogy into the corporate environment, through decentralization, this company succeeded in giving clients control over priorities and better familiarizing I.S. staff with clients' businesses. But they also experienced a number of unnecessary costs, and the I.S. function became significantly less effective.

Here's what happened:

Innovation slowed: By breaking the function into small, decentralized groups, they created a set of "stovepipe" organizations — parallel groups that didn't work with each other. Since each little group had to do everything for its clients, staff could not afford to specialize and focus on building depth in any area of technology. These decentralized generalists found it difficult to keep up with the rapid developments in their profession, so the pace of innovation slowed.

Quality dropped: Generalists lacked the experience of specialists, and could not produce products of equal quality.

Results were fragmented: Each business unit developed its own systems, since sharing with others would have taken time away from its own objectives. And, people did not get together to agree on architectural standards. As a result, there was little chance of collaboration among business units through shared systems.

Costs rose: Each group had to learn everything on its own, and the many parallel learning curves and constant reinvention were very expensive. Costs also rose when generalists struggled to do things that experienced specialists would find easy. And when clients needed someone really good, they looked outside to contractors and outsourcing, which further increased costs.

People were demotivated: Career paths were fragmented. Opportunities for learning new technologies and mastering professional skills diminished. And people's sense of professional identity faded due to a lack of ongoing exchange with colleagues.

It's critically important to trace each issue to the right root causes, that is, to the right organizational systems.

What was the root cause of the clients' dissatisfaction? It was not structure, but rather the internal economy.

There is no reason why clients cannot retain absolute control over what information systems they buy from a centralized I.S. department. The answer is in an internal economy that distributes spending power rather than people. Each business unit could have controlled dollars (or chips representing I.S. staff's time), and, as a result, retained absolute control over what it "eats."

But by using structure (decentralization) to solve a problem whose root cause was the internal economy, the company suffered reduced innovation, lower quality, lost synergies, higher costs, and a demotivated staff. In solving a problem by changing the wrong organizational system, this company paid dearly.

16. A Program of Systematic Change

Analysis of root causes is the centerpiece of RoadMap, a process of systemic change that includes a few simple steps (summarized in Figure 3). These steps can be used to engage a leadership team in a planning process that determines what changes are needed while building their understanding of organizational design and their commitment to change.

Components of Change

Change is not easy, especially fundamental change in the way an organization works.

Effective change is built on three components:

*   Dissatisfaction with the status quo.
*   A vision of the destination.
*   A clear path from here to there.

The RoadMap planning process addresses all three components as it diagnoses an organization's problems and determines a course of action.

Symptoms

The starting point is data collection. As Pat intuited, both client interviews and staff feedback reveal symptoms that need to be addressed. In those symptoms, leaders find evidence of *dissatisfaction with the status quo* — the first component of change — as well as data needed to analyze root causes.

Staff feedback is gathered in an organizationwide meeting carefully designed to engender a safe environment in which people can be open and honest. Participants suggest themes, and then those who

are interested in each theme attend a break-out session on that topic
and brainstorm their concerns. Their comments are gathered into a
document that includes everybody's issues and ideas, and shared
with everybody to be sure they feel heard.

Client feedback is best gained through interviews with key opinion
leaders (not through written surveys which lack depth). The focus
of the discussion should be on clients' feelings about their partnership with the organization and their perception of the strategic value
of its products (but not on specific projects or technical issues).
Again, results are summarized and communicated to participants.

A broader cross-section of clients can also be surveyed in a meeting
like the one in which staff expressed their concerns.

Vision and Gaps

To augment both the dissatisfaction with the status quo and their
understanding of the problems, leaders brainstorms a vision of the
ideal organization.

"Vision statements" are popular, but frequently are of little value.
Vague inspirational mottos that promise a glowing future have
minimal impact. They don't tell people precisely what is expected
of them.

The most powerful way to portray a clear vision is through a set of
specific expectations — the things the organization must do to
succeed. Consider the question, *"What precisely should be
expected (by clients and ourselves) of the ideal organization of the
future?"*

To influence people's day-to-day performance, expectations should
be clear and actionable. And they should be *visionary,* stretching
people to levels of performance well beyond the status quo. (For
thought starters, see Chapter 3.)

By stretching the leadership team to think about what should be
expected of their organization in the future, this workshop

encourages participants to set their sights high — to think about types and levels of performance that otherwise might not have been considered. This establishes a clear *vision of the destination,* one that should be both inspiring and challenging — the second component of change.

As a side benefit, the experience of working together to generate this clear vision helps focus a leadership team on shared goals. Thereafter, communicating the vision can help rally all the staff around common goals.

A practical vision comprises clear, actionable expectations.

After the vision has been documented, the next step is a gap analysis — an assessment of the current performance of the organization against these expectations. This causes leaders to discover that they need to do a lot more than they're doing today, and reaffirms the need for change — the *dissatisfaction with the status quo.*

The gaps also help leaders explain why they believe significant changes are needed. In addition, the gaps augment the database of symptoms to be addressed.

Root-Cause Analysis

All these symptoms — from clients, staff, and the leadership team itself — are then analyzed to determine their root causes. This root-cause analysis is based on the five organizational systems and the subsystems within each.

To identify the real root causes of a symptom, leaders must repeatedly ask the question, "Why? Why would this problem occur?" The answer constitutes a cause. The next question is, "Why would this cause occur?" They continue to ask why until the symptom is traced to one or more of the five fundamental organizational systems.

Any single symptom may be the result of one or more root causes. And the collection of symptoms recognized by clients, staff, and the leadership team typically all emanate from the same few root causes. Therefore, it is not wise to prioritize symptoms; rather, it's better to prioritize root causes and their related solutions.

At the end of this phase of the process, the leadership team is focused on critical *systemic* dysfunctions that are at the core of everbody's concerns.

Corrective Actions

Once root causes are discovered, the most effective and lasting solutions should be apparent.

First, root causes are clustered where appropriate.

For example, all the cultural issues are best treated together in an integrated implementation process. The same is true of structure, where the entire organization must be designed as an integrated system.

Internal economy dysfunctions may be grouped into two or more steps. The first step is to stabilize the current internal economy; subsequent steps can then move it to more advanced stages of evolution. At each step, all four subsystems must be treated, since all are interrelated parts of a total system.

The various methods and tools that are needed are best addressed individually.

Metrics issues may be separated from rewards; but the various concerns related to metrics should be clustered to be sure that the system of metrics is comprehensive.

The clusters of root causes reveal corrective actions, such as structural change or internal economy redesign. Converting clusters of causes to actions is generally just a matter of changing the grammar from a problem (e.g., "our structure lacks these functions") to an action (e.g., "restructure the organization").

Action Planning

The corrective actions are then sequenced into a P.E.R.T. chart. The sequence is partly based on urgency. But it's just as important to take into account the interdependencies among the five organizational systems (described in Chapter 17).

This P.E.R.T. chart — a "RoadMap" — becomes the leadership team's transformational action plan. (An example is given in Figure 4.) The RoadMap satisfies the third component of change — *a clear path from here to there* — i.e., a plan that will take the organization from the status quo to the visionary future.

A RoadMap is an action plan to build a high-performance organization by transforming all the relevant organizational systems.

The RoadMap is a higher level of planning than strategic planning. It is a "meta-plan" that describes a rational, well-paced transformational process to develop an organization that continually succeeds and continually adapts itself to a changing environment.

Communicating the RoadMap

At this point, the leadership team is ready to communicate the RoadMap. Communicating the symptoms tells clients and staff, "We heard you." And communicating the RoadMap itself tells people what changes to expect over what period of time. Investments in communication help build the patience and understanding of both clients and staff that will be needed throughout the rest of the RoadMap process.

First, a document is developed that includes the RoadMap itself, as well as all the symptoms (client feedback, staff input, and the visionary expectations and gaps) along with the root-cause analyses of each.

For something this important, written communication is not enough. A face-to-face presentation of the RoadMap is advisable, complete with plenty of time for questions and discussion.

The presentation is best done as a team effort (rather than solely by the organization's top executive). It might include the following messages:

* We listened to you. Here's what we heard you say: [summary of staff and client feedback].

* We leaders also have concerns. Much more is now expected of us: [overview of visionary expectations]. And while we've been successful in the past, we may not be prepared for these greater challenges in the future [the gaps].

* We've tried a number of organizational improvement programs in the past. They've had a positive effect, and positioned us to tackle a more ambitious program of change. But now we must undertake more widespread change.

* As we go forward, we are committed to systemic change, not just treating the symptoms ("fighting alligators"). This is the time to "drain the swamp." In this spirit, we analyzed the root

causes of each of your and our concerns. [Give an example of a symptom and a train of logic to the root cause.] This analysis is quite detailed, and is documented in the handout.

* We found five broad categories of root causes: [Describe the five systems within organizations and the subsystems within each.]

* We know we can only do so much at once. So we analyzed priorities and interdependencies, and developed a plan of action: [Describe the RoadMap.]

* As a result of this plan, we will see significant changes in coming years. But so long as you remember this "big picture," you'll know what to expect. It won't seem like a series of unrelated "management fads."

* We are all committed to this plan, and we hope that you will join us in this adventure. While we value critical thinking, in the tough road ahead we need your encouragement, involvement, and support. Negativity, cynicism, and closed-mindedness won't do any of us any good, and is not part of the culture that we'd like to create.

* The result of our hard work together will be an organization that satisfies our clients and is the kind of place where we all want to work: one that is highly competitive and earns us all the job security and career growth that come from being part of a successful enterprise.

Generally, this sort of presentation is extremely well received. Although a natural reaction is "to wait and see," virtually everybody feels heard and is aware that their concerns are being taken seriously. And most people believe that their organization is now on a positive path of self improvement.

Implementation

Of course, follow-through is essential. The next step is to implement the RoadMap plan.

Within each step, leaders study the science and methods of the relevant organizational system, and develop detailed implementation plans.

17. The Cart and the Horse

Sequencing corrective actions into a P.E.R.T. chart requires an understanding of the interdependencies among the five organizational systems. It's not wise to sequence corrective actions simply by priority, that is, by the degree of pain that the system is causing. Leaders may not be able to fix the most troublesome system until progress is made on other systems, and doing it first would be putting the cart before the horse.

While every organization is different, some general guidelines apply:

Culture

Most leaders choose to define cultural principles very early in the RoadMap, because a clear understanding of the future style of doing business helps with the design of other systems.

In particular, cultural principles regarding cooperation and teamwork may be prerequisite to structure, since designing a high degree of specialization into the structure bets on effective teaming (influenced by the culture). Cultural principles regarding entrepreneurship and customer focus are key to the design of an effective internal economy.

However, once defined, some portions of the cultural change may have to await changes in the other systems, such as structure. Since there may be systemic barriers to behaving in the new way, some cultural principles may not be actionable until other changes are implemented.

For example, a culture of empowerment (managing by results) depends on a structure that defines jobs by product lines rather than tasks. It does no good to preach empowerment when the structure does not allow people to identify with the products that customers ultimately buy. In such cases, the implementation of a portion of the new culture must wait until the new structure is ready to be announced.

Nonetheless, it is best to plan the entire set of cultural principles together. After they are designed, the leadership team implements those that are feasible right away, and later implements the few remaining principles after other systemic changes are completed.

Structure

Structure is generally tackled very early in the RoadMap. It is an extremely powerful system that establishes the basic outlines of a new organization. It is also a prerequisite to many other changes. For example, the right structural groups must be in place before the methods-tools and metrics-rewards systems can have their full impacts.

Within structure, the two subsystems (the organization chart and work flows) are tightly coupled. An organization chart that clarifies people's focus and enhances specialization is dependent on effective cross-boundary work flows. Conversely, clear definitions of work flows depend on clear boundaries defined by the organization chart. Thus, it's best to consider the two subsystems as a single change process and treat them both at the same time.

Structure is an intensive activity that requires the full attention of the entire management team. It should not be scheduled in parallel with other change efforts.

Internal Economy

Ideally, an adjustment to the internal economy should be scheduled after structure for a number of reasons. An effective Consultancy function in the structure is needed to help clients work out their purchase-decision processes. Furthermore, a comprehensive view of structure defines each group's product lines, a prerequisite to the discipline of contracting. And, in more advanced stages of internal economy where products are priced, the work flows defined in the structure are needed to identify people's "subcontractors," a concept necessary to analyzing prices that cover all direct and indirect costs.

In some cases, however, the internal economy must be treated before structure. For example, if supply and demand are so badly out of balance that people don't have time to think about structure, then some basic work on internal economy may have to come first.

Also, if the staff of an internal service function are divided into groups for each business unit or client community (rather than by their specialty), then the old structure may be serving to give clients a sense of their finite spending power and control over priorities. That is, an aspect of the internal economy has been imbedded in the structure.

In such a case, if leaders restructure an organization around specialties instead of clients (a healthier approach to structure), then the restructuring would dismantle a critical portion of the internal economy. Clients would naturally be quite upset at their loss of control. In these cases, the internal economy must be fixed — to give clients control over spending power rather than a fixed group of people — before the structure can be safely changed.

It may be appropriate to implement a small change in the internal economy before structure, and then a more comprehensive change afterwards. The first treatment of an organization's internal economy generally resolves problems with the current stage of evolution, but does not progress it to a more advanced stage. Later in the RoadMap, another internal-economy project may advance the organization to the next evolutionary stage.

Each organization will have to consider its unique trade-offs before deciding whether to place internal economy before or after structure.

Methods and Tools

Generic methods and tools, which apply to everybody in the organization, can be taught at any time. Their placement in the RoadMap can be based on relative urgency.

Profession-specific methods and tools, on the other hand, are dependent on structure. If there is no "home" for a method — a group that is clearly focused on learning and evolving the method — then training is futile.

Conversely, when structure gives people a clear career focus, they will naturally pursue the best methods within their specialty. Ongoing methods development becomes a natural outcome of a healthy structure. Therefore, profession-specific methods and tools generally should come after structure.

Numerous methods can be introduced in parallel so long as each affects a different profession within the organization.

Metrics and Rewards

Metrics and rewards, like methods, can be sorted into two categories: organizationwide, and profession-specific.

Metrics (and benchmarks) which apply to the entire organization can be done at any time. Early in the RoadMap, they can help people understand what is expected of them, and convince them of the need for change by demonstrating that the status quo is not adequate. They can also help leaders diagnose what changes are needed by defining gaps in performance that become the subject of root-cause analysis.

Organizationwide metrics may be repeated periodically to motivate people throughout the rest of the change process and to measure progress.

Profession-specific metrics are another matter. If done too soon, they make an organization less open to change. It's easy to imagine someone saying, "Don't change the rules on me, boss. I'm trying to make my numbers!"

In fact, since they solidify the status quo, existing metrics and rewards may reinforce old behaviors and make change more difficult. Thus, it may be wise to eliminate existing metrics or weaken their ties to rewards early in the RoadMap process, and replace them later with new metrics tied to new behaviors.

Another problem with metrics done too soon is sub-optimization. If only a few objectives are measured, people will focus on those activities to the exclusion of the other things that they should be doing. To ensure a comprehensive set of metrics, each group must fully understand all the things that it must do. This occurs only after new working patterns have settled into place.

Properly sequencing the steps in the RoadMap is critical to success.

A third problem with premature metrics is subversion. If metrics are installed before people have changed, they tend to find ways to improve the metrics via old behaviors. A common example occurs when companies introduce a sales-force compensation plan intended to bring about new behaviors; somehow, sales people always seem to find a way to continue old behaviors and still make more money!

In general, profession-specific metrics are a way to institutionalize and fine-tune a new organization, not a way to change an organization. As such, they should be done late in the process, after people understand what the right behaviors are and can define all the appropriate objectives to measure.

People respond best to metrics when they directly impact their well-being. Linking rewards to metrics is a way to amplify the power of metrics. Thus, rewards programs should be developed in conjunction with (or after) metrics. Doing rewards programs too soon risks strengthening existing metrics, which may or may not be aligned with the behaviors desired in the new organization.

Overall Timing

Paradoxically, effective leadership requires both a sense of urgency in dealing with current issues, and a patient, persistent, and visionary approach to building a healthy organization.

RoadMap is not a quick fix whose duration is counted in weeks or months. It initiates an ongoing process of systemic change by planning fundamental changes to be implemented over the course of two or three years. After these initial steps are completed, systematic leaders continually update and extend the plan, seeking new opportunities for organizational improvement.

Of course, benefits accrue all along the way. But systematic leadership is a process, not a project that is completed and then forgotten.

If the RoadMap process seems like too much work, there is a way to reduce the impact on leaders' schedules without any loss of quality. The RoadMap process can be stretched over a longer period of elapsed time to reduce the amount of time and money spent per month on transformational efforts.

This is far better than reducing an organization's aspirations, or sacrificing quality and doing a poor job of implementation by taking short cuts. While stretching the elapsed time delays the benefits (and prolongs the pain), at least it does not reduce the eventual quality of the change or add unnecessary risks.

The limiting factor is captured in the concept of "momentum." If too much time goes by between events, people lose sight of the vision of the destination, waste time reminding themselves of what happened in the last event, and become cynical about the lack of progress. There is a delicate balance between "burn-out," on the one extreme, and loss of momentum on the other.

It is far better to stretch the RoadMap process over a longer period of elapsed time than to reduce an organization's aspirations or sacrifice quality.

If people have no time at all to invest in change, they may be temporarily experiencing an unusual level of work load or stress. In this case, it's best to wait a little while before starting the process.

But if current pressures are no worse than usual, people face the classic conundrum: They are too busy fighting alligators to drain the swamp. Of course, while they're fighting a few alligators, the rest of the alligators are breeding! Fighting today's alligators is myopic; it does nothing to prepare an organization for the onslaught of alligators tomorrow. Clearly, draining the swamp is an enlightened leader's highest priority.

There's never a good time to drain the swamp. Leaders must somehow keep their organizations running and still find time to invest in processes that will later save time and put their organizations on a healthy track. In fact, the ability to do just that — to manage priorities and focus attention on a vision and on change — is the difference between a transformational leader and a manager who does no more than maintain the status quo.

Most effective leaders feel a sense of urgency. They want to go fast. But the impatient leader must remember the many person-years it takes to design a high-performance car. A desire to go fast cannot be satisfied by a vehicle designed quickly rather than well.

RESULTS

Far better it is to dare mighty things,
to win glorious triumphs,
even though checkered by failure,
than to take rank with those poor spirits
who neither enjoy much nor suffer much
because they live in the grey twilight
that knows not victory nor defeat.

— Theodore Roosevelt —

18. The Case of the Systematic Leader

The "foreman" in Chapter 6, used as an example of the wrong approach to leadership, was an I.S. executive. As the other bookend, consider the story of a highly effective I.S. executive.

Bill was the C.I.O. in a large petro-chemical firm. He managed a reliable, cost-effective I.S. department, and mid-level managers throughout the corporation were reasonably satisfied with its services.

But Bill recognized trouble on the horizon. Senior executives did not view I.S. as strategic; they were grumbling about costs and unresponsiveness; and some were proposing decentralization and outsourcing.

Meanwhile, people in I.S. were overworked and underappreciated, and had virtually no time to learn new technologies and skills. I.S. provided only limited guidance on architectural standards. Furthermore, the department was failing to recover its costs through chargebacks, a particularly risky position in a corporation that was downsizing.

The symptoms were very much like those which Pat had encountered.

Like Pat, Bill gathered input from key clients and I.S. staff through surveys and interviews. Then he assembled the I.S. management team for a series of workshops.

First, they considered the data — from clients, staff, and themselves. They found four major problem areas: poor relationships with their clients, more work than they could handle, an inadequate pace of technology innovation, and a lack of leadership on technology architecture.

In each case, they analyzed root causes.

The management team traced their poor relationships with client executives to a number of causes:

1. Their *structure* did not include a full-time Consultancy group to serve as account representatives. As a result, executive-level clients didn't understand what the I.S. department was doing for them, and felt ignored.

2. The *culture* did not include the practice of forming clear contracts, which led to misunderstandings over the scope of projects.

3. Executives did not feel that Bill's department was delivering strategic value. Bill's management team recognized that they lacked *methods* of strategic needs assessment to find breakthrough opportunities, and of benefits measurement to justify strategic investments. Since no one had time to study such methods, this was related to the missing Consultancy group (a gap in the *structure*).

4. Complaints about costs, as well as pressures for decentralization and outsourcing, were partially rooted in an *internal economy* that did not give individual business units control over I.S. expenditures. Even though Bill's department charged for its services and clients decided what they would buy, prices were confusing and there were many cross-subsidies. This also made it difficult for I.S. managers to understand and control the end-to-end costs of their products and services.

5. External benchmarks and *metrics* of costs were found to be lacking, so the I.S. department could not prove that it was, indeed, reasonably priced.

The second problem area — more work than they could handle — resulted in an overworked and underappreciated staff and the appearance of unresponsiveness. It was traced to an *internal economy* that failed to balance supply and demand. Prices did not cover the full costs of producing some products, and supply was not allowed to float to meet demand due to artificial caps on headcount and expenses. The lack of clear contracts (a *culture* problem) exacerbated this problem by leading clients to expect more than the department was prepared to deliver.

The third problem area — an inadequate pace of technological innovation — was also traced to the structure and internal economy. In the *structure,* the same people were responsible for both innovation and operations. Facing this conflict of interests, the "keep-things-stable" operational mentality won out and subjugated innovation.

Further constraining innovation, in the *internal economy,* schedules and prices assumed that staff would spend 80 percent of their time on clients' projects, leaving little time for learning. Furthermore, there was no source of "equity" funding to finance new business ventures.

The fourth problem area — the lack of leadership on architectural standards and integration — was attributed to a gap in the *structure* (no full-time architect) and a lack of *methods* for dynamic architecture planning.

In summary, the variety of symptoms were all traced to the five basic organizational systems.

These root causes were then sequenced into an RoadMap that systemically addressed their concerns. As a result of this open and revealing participative process, Bill and the leadership team committed to an ambitious transformational plan that included the following components:

1. They developed cultural principles around themes such as entrepreneurship and customer focus. For example, they said, "We offer our customers alternatives and inform them of the life-cycle costs of each, and then let them choose."

    The culture process began with a workshop to develop cultural principles. This alone had positive impacts on the leaders who attended. Organizationwide training followed.

2. Second, they restructured the department, beginning with a clean sheet of paper. The new structure includes a Consultancy dedicated to client partnership, and an Architect who facilitates consensus on standards. The new structure also separates innovation from operations functions to avoid any conflicts of interests.

This was the most difficult part of the RoadMap. First, the top-level leadership team designed the tier-one structure, i.e., the people who would report directly to Bill. Then, before they turned their attention to the next tier of the organization chart, tier-one leaders worked diligently to develop clear product lines and to understand how real work would flow across organizational boundaries.

After the tier-one leaders fully understood how the new structure would work, tier-two leaders were brought into the process. Tier-one and tier-two leaders worked together to clearly define their boundaries, dividing the tier-one leader's products among them. They, too, practiced "walk-throughs" to learn how cross-boundary teams would form to handle a variety of kinds of projects.

By the time they had assigned the entire staff and prepared the announcement, all the leaders understood their respective lines of business and how they would work together in many different situations. This allowed them to work as a team on the announcement. Together, they produced a half-day, worldwide video teleconference followed by afternoon small-group meetings.

In a series of subsequent meetings, they trained staff at every level. Finally, everyone in the department was involved in migrating commitments to the appropriate places in the newly structured organization.

3. Once the structure was deployed, leaders developed and trained the staff in leading-edge methods. Consultants learned how to identify strategic opportunities, and how to measure the so-called "intangible" benefits. Architects learned an evolutionary, participative method of standards planning that is quite different from the typical top-down plan.

4. Then, the leadership team began to work on the internal economy. Since the department had worked for a long time in a full-chargeback environment, they didn't feel the need to do a thorough analysis of the internal economy. But they did need to align their resources with their newly-defined product lines and bring down their costs.

    To drive this, they identified a set of product managers responsible for all the costs of each of their major product lines. These product managers began to sort costs into the right products, and improved time tracking to get better data on their costs. They unraveled pricing subsidies to avoid selling some products at a loss, and monitored product revenues and costs. By focusing on product-line profitability, they found many opportunities for streamlining and savings.

5. When the new organization began working well, the leadership team felt ready to stand up to external comparisons. To head off an outsourcing threat, they benchmarked their costs (favorably) against competitors, and advertised the results to client executives.

While Bill recognizes that there is still more to do, the results so far have been impressive. Complaints have dwindled, and client executives are much more satisfied with the department. Partnerships with clients have improved, and many business units have now invited the I.S. Consultants to become involved in their strategic planning processes.

Now, clients understand the business value of architecture and are enthusiastically supporting standardization. In fact, many are demanding that their suppliers (both the department and its competitors) comply with architectural standards, and they're willing to pay for it. This gave the Architects a great deal of credibility with internal Technologists.

Internal processes have been streamlined, costs have dropped by 15 percent, and in spite of reducing their prices by 2 percent, the department is close to its breakeven goal. Equally important, client executives were impressed by the benchmarks, and pressures for decentralization and outsourcing have diminished.

The highest praise came from one business unit — Bill's largest customer — in the form of a contract with Bill's corporate I.S. department to take over their distributed computing support (formerly decentralized). Another corporate service function — Finance — is now analyzing how to merge its decentralized I.S. staff into Bill's department.

Clearly, the best indication that an organization is fundamentally healthy is in its ability to win market share through superior performance.

19. The Payoff

The results of the RoadMap process are felt at three levels: the benefits of the planning process, the benefits of the plan, and the benefits of implementing the plan. A quick look at the potential benefits of each can help leaders get the most from their efforts.

Benefits of the Planning Process

The RoadMap planning process engages a leadership team in self-analysis and participative planning. Leaders study the science and methods within each organizational system, understand every concern and analyze its root causes, create a shared vision of the organization of the future, and develop detailed implementation plans for systemic change.

Unlike an external consultant's report, participation takes advantage of insiders' understanding of the issues, and generates a consensus on the need for change. Working together as a leadership team on this process establishes a foundation of common language and frameworks, and rallies everyone around shared goals. As a result, the planning process is effective, educational, and a tremendous team-building experience.

Benefits of the Plan

The RoadMap plan alone has significant value. Because it focuses efforts at the systemic rather than symptomatic level, the plan describes a thorough treatment of complex and interrelated organizational issues. This ensures that changes don't cause other problems, and that they lead to solutions that last.

RoadMap also puts corrective actions in the proper order, avoiding the common frustration of change efforts rendered ineffective because prerequisite changes have not been made.

RoadMap links changes directly to people's concerns. This linkage from symptoms to root causes tells people exactly how each of their concerns will be addressed. Working the linkage the other way, people can see what the expected benefits of each change will be. Thus, staff understand that leaders are responding to their concerns, and see what each of the changes will do for them.

There are benefits to the RoadMap planning process, to the plan, and to implementing the plan.

Perhaps most importantly, the plan allows people to understand that changes are not isolated "experiments," or another "management fad of the month." Rather, the RoadMap shows staff that each change is part of an integrated, systemic plan.

Communicating the plan explains that the organization is headed for success, without unrealistically expecting any single change to be the "silver bullet" that solves every problem. This instills confidence that RoadMap will build the kind of organization in which people want to work.

Benefits of Implementing the Plan

Of course, implementing the plan delivers all the benefits of a healthy organization. These benefits are at two levels:

*   The performance of the organization.
*   The organization's ability to adapt to a changing environment.

High-performance organizations bring out the best in everyone. People prosper in supportive, empowered work environments. Whether they work individually or on teams, their efforts automatically mesh. Motivated, effective, and coordinated people ensure their clients' satisfaction. With happy clients, organizations grow, providing both career opportunities to staff and synergies beneficial to clients. In this way, success feeds on success.

With every bright mind engaged, healthy organizations automatically adapt to shifts in clients' strategies, technologies, and market threats and opportunities.

Systemic change is a good investment in another way as well. When the five organizational systems are well aligned, everybody continually looks for new ways to improve their work. With every bright mind engaged, healthy organizations automatically adapt to shifts in clients' strategies, technologies, and market threats and opportunities. This alleviates the need for continual management intervention and costly reorganizations.

In every aspect of both their work and their adaptive processes, the RoadMap puts organizations on an upward spiral to success.

20. Dynamic Organizations
Need Dynamic Leaders

To prosper in challenging times, organizations must be dynamic. They must innovate, align themselves with diverse clients' strategies and market opportunities, improve internal processes for project delivery and operations, and integrate their products. And they must do all these things simultaneously (not one at a time as special projects), and do them all continually (not once a year as part of an annual plan or occasionally when executives initiate task forces).

Executives who try to personally coordinate and control everything are destined to fail (and are likely candidates for ulcers as well). The proper role for an executive is that of leader, not foreman — one who focuses on issues of governance rather than projects and crises.

When problems arise, an executive must solve them. But the true leader doesn't stop there. He or she asks, "Why did this problem rise to my level in the first place? And how can we fix the root cause so the problem doesn't happen again?"

Focusing on systemic change gives an executive the leverage he or she needs to handle the tremendous pace and complexity of today's business challenges. By consciously designing the organizational environment that guides everybody in every aspect of their work, a leader can subtly influence every decision, every day — without disempowering and micro-managing people.

Through systemic change, leaders can build healthy, high-performance organizations that succeed . . . with or without them.

Index